I0020035

The Dark Side of the Hacking World

What You Need to Know to Guard Your Precious Assets and Remain Safe

By Mike Mason

WE CANT BE BEAT LLC

Table of Contents

3

Introduction

As you read these words, someone somewhere is stealing someone's password, their personal data, or even their entire identity. Someone is turning into an overnight millionaire with just a few easy clicks, and leaving their unwitting victims penniless, shocked, and confused.

How, you may ask?

The answer is so simple that it surprises a lot of people—through hacking. You may never have thought of yourself as a prime target for a hack attack, but I'm here to tell you right now that you definitely are. Although many people believe they're safe because they don't go online much, or even because they "have nothing to hide", it's a well-known fact that whether you connect for 5 minutes a day or 15 hours a day, you're equally at risk. And as for hackers not having anything to gain from watching your movements—did you know that your Social Security number, or your full name and date of birth alone are enough to net hackers a tidy profit and leave your life shattered in the process? Everyone has something worth protecting; everyone has something they can't afford to let hackers steal.

But not everyone understands how to stop them from doing so.

Knowledge is power and in this era of ultra-advanced technology, where millions upon millions of people exchange information in just one click, you can NOT afford to ignore the dark side of the web. The fact is, whether for good or for bad, we are all living in a highly connected world and our entire lives are accessible at the fingertips of total strangers.

In this kind of world, the less you know about the hacking world and its shadowy techniques, the more vulnerable you are to being attacked, having your vital personal information held for ransom, or even being watched and followed by cyber-criminals!

When you understand hacking tricks, techniques, risks and maneuvers, you are placing yourself in a winning position. That's why it's so vital that you know about the world of hacking and the secrets it holds. Lack of knowledge is weakness and leads to vulnerability. To put it simply, internet connectivity is the way of the future and knowledge of hacking gives YOU the key to that future.

When it comes to the internet and hacking, ignorance is not bliss. It's just plain dangerous!

That's why I have created this book. To help you defeat your enemy, the hacker, by knowing everything you can about hacking. Consider it a manual, a guide to help steer you through the basics of hacking and to help you understand just what it is that so many hackers are doing out there that is turning them into overnight successes.

The world of hacking is not like anything you've ever imagined. Many people think of a hacker as a geeky, lonely teenage boy on his computer day and night, just trying to cause trouble. This couldn't be further from the truth. These days, hackers are the new kings and robber barons of our time. Where once, big business was the place to make your millions, today, even the most basic hacking skills can help you make literally millions of dollars in a very short space of time, while leaving a trail of unsuspecting targets in your wake.

This is the reality we live in now. That's why it is so important that you fully understand these tricks and have the knowledge to use this information for your own benefit, rather than letting mastermind hackers use it AGAINST you.

This guide is packed with all of this information including detailed information about the lucrative underworld of hacking, the different types of hackers to watch out for, the numerous tools and dangerous schemes they could use against you, PLUS useful tutorials that lay open every step of some of the most damaging hacks that hackers employ and expert advice to help you equip, prepare and protect yourself from these attacks.

It is a window into the amazing secrets of the hacking world, giving you a clear view of what so many millions of people will never know about the shocking techniques and easy steps that turn normal everyday Joe's into the top hackers in the world!

Are you ready to clear away your vague ideas about hacking and learn the surprising truth? Are you ready to stop worrying about potential hacks against you and start knowing exactly how to see them coming from a mile off and defend yourself from them?

If so, join me in chapter 1 where we'll be dismissing common misconceptions and revealing the facts behind the hacking world.

Let's get started!

Chapter 1:
An Introduction to the Secret World of Hacking and the Hacker Next Door

1. Introduction To Hacking

What is hacking? If asked to answer this question, the majority of people wouldn't really have a clear response. That's because the hacking world, though often shown in movies and mentioned on the news, is actually a very secretive world. Its survival depends on its ability to close itself off from outsiders and defy any attempts at definition, identification, or infiltration. From naturally gifted amateurs, young prodigies, and technology aficionados, to ethical hackers and dangerous cyber-criminals, hackers are impossible to classify under just one banner. For the purposes of this book, however, I'm going to be focusing on the hackers who directly threaten the safety, livelihoods, and security of millions of people around the world, who could at this very moment be entering your private files, draining your hard earned money, listening in on your conversations, or even worse, watching you.   While it's certainly important to know about the other various types of hackers and their motivations, the magnitude of damage caused by hackers with unscrupulous goals and methods has reached a point where ignoring them would be foolish.

The dangers posed by malicious hackers are growing exponentially, and people who mistakenly believe that an outdated anti-virus and a general knowledge of internet safety will be enough to keep them secure are in serious trouble. That's why I wrote this book—as an urgent wake-up call to the millions who go online every single day and go about their daily work and entertainment without realizing that at every moment, and at every click, someone could be watching, just waiting to pounce.

The days when we could leave our online security in the hands of others are long gone. Today, with even young kids joining the ranks of malicious hackers, you simply cannot afford to avoid the truth: The web has a very dark side, and the kingpins who rule that side are always in the background, dropping in on your social media posts, noticing your location, your profession, and even the names of your friends and family. They are looking for the weakest possible target to launch a hack campaign on, and if you don't know enough about THEIR world, THEIR tools, and THEIR tricks, they could end up seriously affecting YOUR life. With this in mind, I invite you to use the information in this book to guide you, to give you an opening into the shadowy, dark side of the hacking world, and how to keep yourself your loved ones and all of your valuable data and assets safe from the total havoc that malicious hackers can unleash.

Now, of course, I would never make the claim or even believe the claim that any one tool, book, guide, or technique can guarantee your safety. Hackers by nature love to look for new and unheard of ways into your systems, and will try continually until they make a hit. However, no matter how cunning, how methodical, or how persistent these hackers may be, equipping yourself with the right information about them and their scams and exploits is the only real way to protect what you have and keep it out of their dangerous hands.

In order to ensure that you get a complete view of the hacking world, I'll be providing you with a full background of hacking, including its history, reasons for its existence, tools and other details that will immediately give you a better handle on the hacking secrets you need to know.

2. Hacking Explained

The term "hacking" has become another word for any form of clever, unorthodox technical work on a system or device, not necessarily related to computers. You often hear people these days mention the term in a positive, creative context such as: "Amazing furniture hacks you never thought of" or "easy ways to hack calculus". A large portion of society views hacking as mere problem solving. This is, in part, due to a lack of understanding about the rising dangers of hacking.

Hacking's true definition is actually closer to the act or process of criminal (or less than above board) computer manipulation or computing activity. Hackers gain unauthorized access to computer systems through various methods that include breaking passwords, bypassing security and cracking codes. In essence, they go where they have not been invited, using methods that are not allowed.

Although some hackers really are hacking just for the fun of it, if a malicious hacker gains the ability to exploit a weakness in your system and hacks you, it is anything but enjoyable or harmless.

3. A Brief History Of Hacking

While it is widely believed that hacking is a relatively new and modern phenomenon, the truth is that hacking and hackers have been around for about as long as computers have. The early emergence of hacking can be traced all the way back to the MIT campus in 1961. In that year, MIT got the very first PDP-1 machine and members of a university tech model club were immediately drawn to the device. They quickly began creating programming tools and new methods of utilizing the device, in the process inventing some of the "hacker slang" that is still in use now. In fact, it is thought that MIT was the first place where the term "hacker" was coined in its current sense.

In the late 1960's, scientists such as Ken Thompson at AT&T Bell Labs developed UNIX. This operating system was one of the very first in the world and would go on to become extremely important to both the internet in general and hacking in particular. By 1978, Randy Suess and Ward Christenson had created the very first computer bulletin board system. This allowed hackers to finally link up with another and resulted in the emergence of a private cyberspace.

This development occurred around the same time as the popularity of "phreaking" was rising. "Phreaking" involved groups of early American hackers who tinkered with the national telephone system, in order to find new, useful and interesting ways of utilizing it. By the early 1970s these pioneering hackers had figured out that whistling at the specific pitch of 2600-hertz would allow them illicit entry into the long-distance switching system belonging to AT&T. With this free access, these early hackers enjoyed making international calls and playing with the system. John Draper (also known as "Cap'n Crunch") was a well-known "phreaker", notorious for his surprising discovery that the toy whistles packaged as giveaways inside cereal boxes were perfect for creating just the right pitched whistle to access the network.

Some "phreakers" also made large sums of money by offering this access to those wishing to make cheap international phone calls. They charged each customer for providing entry into the network.

John Draper's legacy in early hacking didn't end with his whistle-discovery. He would go on to create a "blue box" that provided access to the phone network, an invention that fascinated a pair of other early hackers- the famous Steve Jobs and Steve Wozniak.

The early 1980s

By the time the 1980s rolled around, people had access to personal computers, connected by telephone. Hacking enjoyed a hey-day, with young hackers cracking various systems solely for the pleasure of understanding them. By 1986, computer viruses were already a threat and breaking into computer systems was finally deemed to be illegal. With the advent of the Mosaic WWW browser in 1993, hackers begin to share their codes, tips and hacks with each other on the Web.

In 1995, Kevin Mitnick's arrest aroused public interest in the world of hacking, drawing a whole new generation to it. "Spamming" began to occur frequently at about the same time, bringing organizations to their knees with a flood of fake information requests.

By the late 90s, everyone and everything was running on computers and large, powerful hacking groups such as Lopht claimed that they had the power to knock the internet out in less than an hour. The hacking threat of science fiction had finally become all too real. From that point on, hackers were breaking into banks, making away with money and personal data, wreaking havoc on companies with hack campaigns and sending computer viruses to their unsuspecting targets.

It was at this stage that people began to be personally attacked by hackers and the concept of computer security was born.

4. Hackers' Favorite Operating Systems

Different hackers use a variety of operating system types. They are unlikely to use Mac OS because of a lack of available tools and the difficulty involved in porting the tools that are available. Hackers generally utilize the UNIX platform, with a heavy leaning towards the Unix-like Linux. There are several reasons for this choice. One of the primary reasons lies in price. Whether a hacker is hacking for profit or other purposes, keeping costs down is a basic concern. Because Linux is 100% free and open source, it can be used by anyone to view each of the Linux kernel's lines of code. Another reason to use Linux is its extreme simplicity. It provides hackers with the ability to pull off major feats, using only a shell prompt and keyboard, if necessary. And because hackers can access the whole code, Linux can be manipulated by expert hackers to do a vast variety of things it wasn't strictly created for, making it the perfect hacker's playground.

Black hat hackers in particular, adore Linux for the opportunity and flexibility it provides to their malicious creativity. In fact, these hackers often understand Linux far more deeply and intricately than its own producers and they've found it to be secure, strong and stable. Unlike other operating systems, Linux doesn't need regular reboots and rarely slows down, even over long periods of time. This make Linux perfectly suited for malicious hackers, who need their tools to always be sharp and ready for the next massive hacking campaign.

Now that we've gone into the background information necessary to understand hacking, let's delve deeper in the next section and following chapters, taking an up close and personal look behind the screen at the hackers of the dark web and their motivations, skills and methods. In the part 2 of this chapter, join me as I uncover one of the biggest security threats that most people never even suspect!

Chapter 1 Part 2:
The Hacker Next Door
- How the Average Jane or
Joe Could be Your Worst
Security Nightmare!

You know that friendly neighbor who always stops to say hello? What about that work colleague you don't really know that well that you found lurking near your desk? Think about that acquaintance who suddenly asked if they could use your device to fire off a quick email, since theirs was low on batteries. All of these people are potential hackers. If you are having a hard time believing it, consider this:

That friendly neighbor could easily hack into your Wi-Fi network and use it to spy on your every move, on and offline. That colleague you don't know all that well, lurking around your desk, could have been there looking for information about you that he or she could use for a social engineering attack on you or your contacts.

And that acquaintance that you allowed to use your device for "a moment"- well, he or she could have been installing a keystroke logger that would send each click and every single letter you type straight to him or her. The chilling fact is that the hacking threat no longer comes only from an ominous stranger in China or Eastern Europe or from a shadowy gang of hackers who chose your system from an algorithm.

With the rise of shareable technology and tutorials and the growing popularity of hacking in general, the hacker next door has become a dangerous reality, and it's time to protect yourself!

If you've ever been the victim of a targeted hack campaign, you were probably panicked, afraid, angry and confused-wondering who would want to do such a thing and why targeted you. Internet myths tell us that hacking victims are usually chosen at random, as hackers search for vulnerable people and systems to exploit and that it really is a case of being in the "wrong place at the wrong time". Let me tell you right now that, as far as targeted hacks are concerned, I don't believe this popular myth for a minute.

When a hacker chooses you out of millions of potential targets, takes the trouble and care necessary to send you a plausible, trustworthy-sounding email or link and knows just the right tactics to use to make you believe it's from a reliable source-there's NOTHING random about all of that.

You have been watched and carefully chosen out of a vast pool of possible victims, and very often, there is a specific reason behind it. Now, as soon as most people find out they've been hacked, they usually scroll through a mental list of people they know, discarding each possibility because "He doesn't look like a hacker" or "She doesn't seem very techy, there's no way she could have planned and executed this hack".

 As I keep stressing throughout this whole book, it's vital to know that there is no one set type of hacker. They come in as many variations of professions, ages, genders and even skill levels as you, me and other people. They usually don't advertise their abilities in public, although they may boast to other fellow hacker in online forums about their exploits. And remember that just because someone doesn't appear to be a computer whiz, a tech genius or seem to possess any tech skills beyond the bare minimum, that DOESN'T rule them out from being a potential hacker.

Hackers who focus mainly on "cracking" or breaking into systems, devices and networks often do have advanced computer skills such as programming but you can become a malicious hacker without substantial programming or other computer skills. Self-taught hackers frequently purchase already written or created exploits online from advanced hackers. All they have to do is follow a simple step-by-step routine and they can easily install a malicious backdoor executable onto your device remotely. In fact, I will be showing you just how easy mounting this kind of hack can be for beginners, in a later chapter of this book!

So, the important things to take away from this are that A)the hacker may be someone you know who has purposely picked you out for a targeted hack and B)There are many levels of hacking knowledge and a beginner "script kiddie" hacker with little to no real understanding of the intricacies of hacking can do just as much damage(if not more) to your privacy, security, identity, finances and your device, as an advanced hacker who creates all of his or her own exploits.

So what can you do if you believe that you may have been targeted by someone you know? First and foremost, follow the security protocols that I'll be outlining in this book and use them as your guide to prevent and defend yourself against any type of hack. Secondly, back up all of your files because you never know where the hack may lead. Thirdly, stop sending any sensitive data online from the device or network you believe may have been hacked. This goes for particularly confidential activities like online banking, making online payments of any kind and even holding private conversations through messaging. Fourth, remember that hacking is illegal and that your rights CAN be protected. Gather evidence and present it to the relevant authorities as soon as possible. It may mean the difference between safety and losing all of your money, your reputation, your privacy and even your identity!

Chapter 2:
Know Your Enemy -
Understanding Hackers

One of the major maxims of life is that to conquer something, you must first be able to fully understand it. That's why in this chapter we will be taking a close in-depth look at hackers, who they are, the different types of hackers out there, their goals, objectives and methods.

I'm not exaggerating when I say that hacking knowledge is literally the most valuable currency of the future and tat hackers who possess this knowledge are positioned to affect and shape all of our lives in many important ways. Hacking isn't something that you can ignore because it is a cold hard reality of connectivity. Simply closing your eyes to it will only put you in more danger, just like the ostrich that buries its head in the sand to avoid seeing a predator. Basically, it's a hacker's world and everyone else is just living in it. So without further ado, let's delve into the origins, motivations, techniques and secrets of these shady kingpins of the dark web.

The Lineup: The Primary Types of Hackers and What You Need to Know About Each of Them

The popular idea of a hacker is either a dark, shadowy figure hiding behind a computer screen all day or a young, tech-obsessed geeky type who has no life besides hacking simply for the sake of it. Most people couldn't tell you exactly what a hacker is and what hackers do. The truth is that there as many variations of hackers as there are of people and believing in only one stereotype is a sure-fire way of getting burned.

The one thing that you need to know right away is that the many different types of hackers work towards vastly different goals. Knowing this is the first step to uncovering the secrets of the underground web and to protecting yourself from hacks.

Hacker: A hacker is someone with a serious interest in the inner workings of computer operating systems who frequently learns about new vulnerabilities and holes within these systems. Many programmers often become hackers and are already equipped with knowledge of computer operating systems and programming languages. Hackers used to be known as "renegade scientists" of the computer world and were known to only be interested in collecting information and freely sharing their discoveries with others.

Today however, with the huge amount of money to be made in the hacking world and the growing connectivity of modern life, malicious and dangerous hackers far outnumber the "good" ones. These hackers may or may not be into the "science of hacking" but they are definitely engaged in breaking and illegally entering into private systems, destroying the integrity of devices and the data they hold, either for the thrill of it or for financial gain.

While the Hollywood version of a hacker is often a teenage male who likes to play around on computers but according to statistics, the true hacker is much more likely to be any male or female between the ages of 20 to 50 years old who has a real understanding of and dedication to hacking(whether for good or bad).

The Knowledge Hacker

These are the extremely intelligent variety of hacking experts. They do it for the love of knowledge and in order to liberate knowledge form the "few" and disperse it to the "masses". This type of hacker is very unlikely to hack into your system in order to retrieve your data and use it to, say, blackmail you for money. Instead, he or she will be more focused on learning from the very act of infiltrating your system itself and adding to the collective knowledge of the population. Unless you're a major organization hiding secrets or a tech company that wants to keep your newly developed technology under wraps, you have absolutely nothing to fear directly from these very high-minded and intellectual hackers. However, because they create so many of the software scripts and exploits that beginner hackers and malicious hackers use, although they may not mean to cause harm to you or your device, their inventions can be used against you.

These hackers aren't in the hacking game for money, prestige or bragging rights. Instead, they would actually prefer to remain unnamed and unknown. They tend to work independently, staying in the shadows and keeping their activities to themselves.

Ethical Hackers: An ethical hacker (also known as a white hat) is a hacker who possesses all of the same high level skills and breaking in knowledge of a regular hacker but uses these skills for good. They are the self-appointed heroes of the web and the only reason they will break into a system is in order to find and fully explore unknown weaknesses in the system's defenses. Once they find these weaknesses, ethical hackers do not use them to exploit the owner of the device or to damage or destroy any data. Instead, they hand over their findings to the owners of the system and tell them how they can better protect themselves from hacking in the future. Ethical hackers hack for the greater good and do not pose a threat to your device's safety or the security of your private information.

Both knowledge hackers and ethical hackers used to be in the majority, but recently, there have been some disturbing developments. The emergence of the dark web, an unregulated wild west of the internet, where rules don't apply and big money can be made and lost in the blink of an eye, has meant that we are now facing a new breed of unethical hackers. These are your biggest enemies and knowing as much about them as possible will help you to fight them off:

The Black Hat Hacker

If you've ever watched a Western cowboy movie, you've probably noticed that the good guys in the film generally wear white hats while the" bad" characters tend to wear black hats. This is where the term "black hat" hacker comes from. Black hat hackers are the kind of hackers that you really don't want entering your system. They are highly skilled, super-fast and are definitely hacking for purely unethical purposes. Black hat hackers are defined as hackers who break down computer security for malicious reasons or in order to gain benefits of some kind.

Black hat hackers are often to be found forming dangerous criminal hacking rings like the kind we see portrayed in movies. They are constantly working to find vulnerabilities in the systems of private citizens and major organizations. Unlike ethical "white hat" hackers these cyber-criminals then use the information they find not for knowledge purposes, or to help create security patches but in order to enter these systems and get what they want from them. Black hat hackers have formed ruthless hacking groups around the world that are responsible for "ransom" hacks, blackmailing, utilizing your own device against you, in order to secretly watch and record you, emptying bank accounts, stealing people's social security numbers and entire identities and bringing major companies to their knees with coordinated (DoS)Denial of Service campaigns.

What makes these hackers especially dangerous is that they have no rules or code of ethics, are organized purely for profit and are usually very skillful and adept at utilizing social engineering ploys. They get their hands on the exploits created by sophisticated elite hackers and then twist and modify these exploits to use them for illegal, illicit and extremely harmful purposes. Because they are without doubt, the most threatening citizens of the computer underground, we will focus a great deal on the activities these black hat hackers are involved in, how they can harm your devices and your life and what you can do to fight back, within this book.

The Anarchist Hacker: An anarchist hacker is one that wants to damage computer systems and data and bring about disruption, by any means possible. Unlike ethical hackers, these kinds of hackers want to access the private information on your computer and will then use this sensitive to try to destroy your computer or disrupt your life. Often, they will feed off of the approval of other hackers so the more damage they cause to your computer or life, the more recognition and fame they'll get from other unethical hackers and the prouder they will be of themselves. These hackers believe in chaos and will try to unleash as much chaos on your system as possible.

The Script Kiddie Hacker: "Script kiddies" are what the hacking community calls non-technologically advanced rookie hackers who don't really understand computer operating systems or hacking. Instead, these amateurs have just happened to stumble upon some programs and utilities online and are using these tools without knowing much about the technology behind them. This is why they're called "script kiddies". They're not really hacking but just following a pre-set script and because they're not advanced, they are considered immature in the hacking world.

Just like anarchist hackers, script kiddies get their thrills from the kudos of other script kiddies like themselves. They are generally disliked and not respected among other more advanced hackers and are not even considered real full-fledged hackers in the first place. These individuals are often teens and pre-teens and are regarded as annoying amateurs by the wider hacking community.

The truth is that most people think that they know the internet but in reality, there is a whole world out there that is far beyond the average person's understanding. If you only use the internet for email, social media and other "basic" activities, then you're only seeing the very tip of the iceberg.

Black hat hackers, (the malicious hackers who basically run and own the deep web), are the select few who actually know and utilize the internet fully. To know just what is possible in this dark, murky world, you must understand what motivates these hacker/crackers. The main point of unethical black hat hacking lies in the money- using skill and effort, it's possible to make millions in a career as a black hat hacker. Because of this, most malicious hackers are completely devoid of any moral objections and will do whatever it takes to break down your system's security, entering your device, your accounts and even peeking into your home, in order to get the huge financial pay-offs they seek.

Now that we've detailed the primary types of hackers you should be watching out for on the dark web, make sure to join me in the next chapter where I'll introduce you to the most skilled, dangerous and infamous hackers in history and give you a look into their risky, often incredibly lavish lifestyles!

Chapter 3:
Know Your Enemy Part 2
- The Black List:
Lamborghinis, Mansions and
$100,000 a Month Paychecks

Meet The Greatest and Most Dangerous Hackers of All Time!

No book about the dark side of the hacking world would be complete without an introduction to the cunning and extremely brilliant hackers that have rocked the world with their knowledge and techniques. While there are many varieties of hackers out there today, the people we are going to examine are the best and brightest of the dark web- with tricks, scams and reputations that are larger than life!

Allow me to introduce you to the hackers who revolutionized the world of hacking and made everyone reconsider the entire concept of security. Meet the blacklist.

Kim Dotcom: The Mega-Hacker with Worldwide Celebrity Status

Born: 1974

Known Aliases: "Kim Schmitz", "Kimble" or "Kim Tim Jim Vestor"

No hacker in history has had the power to become a household name, with the glitzy cache of a celebrity and the mind of a money-making malicious hacker extraordinaire, except for Kim Dotcom.

Hacker M.O.: Growing up in Germany as Kim Schmitz, Dotcom had an unhappy childhood. In his formative years, he quickly made a name for himself with his daring exploits. His ability to hack into the security of virtually "hack-proof" organizations such as NASA and Citibank made him famous. He became known for breaching the most beefed up security protocols as well as for hacking into numerous Private Bank Exchange (PBX) systems, the access codes for which he sold for a minimum of $200 apiece. In fact, he found entering these systems so easy that he often claimed they were like walking through open doors for him. By 1994, he had already racked up 11 counts of computer fraud and many other hacking charges and was on the fast track to becoming a serious hacking threat. By the early 2000s, Dotcom had done well enough financially to be able to buy nearly half a million dollars' worth of shares in the dying company Letsbuyit.com.

Having heavily publicized this investment and another planned investment in the company, Dotcom sat back and waited as shares of the company spiked to new heights. Then he shrewdly sold his own shares and walked away with a cool $1.63 million. Luckily for him, this wasn't exactly illegal in Germany at the time and he was able to get away with nothing more than a suspended sentence, but it was an early glimpse of Dotcom's money-making genius and ability to outsmart the legal system.

Money, Power and Fame-The Megaupload Life: His hacking abilities appeared to have given him unprecedented access to both the money and private data of various large and respected corporations and organizations. He quickly moved from black hat hacking to making money off his talents by showing major companies like Lufthansa the secret vulnerabilities that other hackers could use against them. From there, he went on to try his hand at internet startups.

He made so much money from the internet that he actually changed his name to Kim Dotcom, in order to pay homage to his source of wealth. Due to the many skills and business acumen he built up as a precocious young hacker, Dotcom was able to branch out into many other ventures, including the gigantic Megaupload file hosting service, which at one point, became the 13th most popular website on the internet and netted an incredible $175 million in revenues.

At the height of its operations, the site was the source of almost 5% of all web traffic and boasted over 50 million visitors to it per day. The young man with the black hat hacker roots had turned into a multi-million dollar wonder with everything from his own helicopters and yachts to the sprawling $24 million dollar mega Dotcom mansion, top models and lavish parties to show for it. Dotcom fleet of exotic vehicles ran the gamut of top brands and he frequently stayed in $12,000 a night hotel suites when traveling. He also thought nothing of spending over $1million to charter a 240- yacht. He then moored this yacht in Monte Carlo and held opulent parties for a wide variety of well-known big names, from celebrities and business tycoons to Prince Rainier of Monaco.

Charges: Unfortunately for Kim Dotcom, all of the wealth he had amassed from hacking and subsequent business ventures wasn't enough to keep him safe from charges of copyright violations, stemming from customer usage of his Megaupload site. Megaupload was thought to be behind at least half a billion dollars in losses and damage for the entertainment industry because the site's over 150 million users were believed to be sharing pirated content illegally.

This led to Dotcom being arrested in a shocking and dramatic arrest that included law enforcement swooping down on the Dotcom mansion and storming the home to find Dotcom in his safe room. A long court battle ensued and Dotcom continues to fight extradition, denying all charges against him. In the meantime, he has gone on to create Mega, a cloud storage and file hosting service that offers its users the ultimate in online security, using encryption to keep all materials safe from prying eyes.

Kim Dotcom's tale highlights the power of the hacking mindset. His rags to unbelievable riches life story serves to show how hackers can harness the abilities and skill sets they gain from hacking to create multi-million dollar opportunities and completely change the way users view and make use of the internet.

Albert Gonzalez: The $200 Million Damage Hacker

Born: 1981

Known Aliases: "Cumbajohny", "Soupnazi", "Segvec", "Kingchilli" and "Stanozlolz"-

When you imagine one of the most successful financial cyber-crime bosses in the world, you probably picture an Ivy League math whiz with an advanced technology degree and tons of formal training, right? Well, the truth is actually very different.

Self-taught American computer hacker Alberto Gonzalez masterminded some of the largest credit card theft hacks in the history of hacking. Gonzalez got his first computer at the tender age of 8 and began experimenting with technology early on. By the age of 14, Gonzalez was already in hot water with the authorities for allegedly hacking into NASA.

With only a high school education and no formal training to speak of, in a few short years, Gonzalez went from being the leader of a rag-tag group of computer geeks at his South Miami high school to being a top level member and eventual kingpin of the ShadowCrew, one of the most prolific hacking teams that the internet ever witnessed. Gonzalez and the ShadowCrew successfully stole and sold nearly millions of credit card numbers and ATM numbers, rocking the financial world to its core and raking in major money!

Hacker M.O.: His rise to power and wealth was accomplished by his genius use of SQL injection techniques to place backdoors into the systems of major corporations. These surreptitious backdoors would then launch ARP spoofing campaigns, opening the door for Gonzalez and his cohorts to rob computer information from these corporations. Using these techniques Gonzalez managed to inflict at least $200 million of financial damage to these corporations and the targets of his hacks. With a talent for deception and an ability to understand both human nature and the intricacies of financial crime, Gonzalez was truly a leading black hat hacker.

Operating out of Kearny, New Jersey, the shadowcrew.com website played host to the roaring business of online credit card hacking, offering hackers the opportunity to register with the site in order to purchase people's stolen account numbers. At its height, shadowcrew.com was basically an eBay for cyber-criminals looking to get in on the massive paydays of credit card fraud and had members from all over Asia, Europe and the United States.

They were also allowed to access numerous step-by-step tutorials, which detailed the art of stealing credit card, ATM card and debit card numbers for resale or illicit use. This made the website immensely popular with cyber-criminals with a particular interest in credit card fraud and theft and Gonzalez was widely regarded as an expert and leader in the field.

Those who became members of this hidden community were also able to participate in massive auctions, allowing them to bid for over 18 million email accounts, passwords, usernames and other pieces of private data that could help them to pull off an identity theft scam.

Gonzalez involved other hacking groups such as Darkprofits and Carderplanet and this led to law enforcement teams from as far afield as Belarus, Bulgaria, Sweden, Canada and the Netherlands hunting down Gonzalez and his crew. In less than 2 years, Gonzalez managed to hack into major companies' systems making away with nearly 50 million debit and credit cards. By hacking into companies such as Office Max, Barnes & Noble, TJ Maxx, DSW, BJ'S Wholesale Club and Sports Authority, Gonzalez made a hacking fortune.

On the surface, he appeared to live very modestly, owning simple homes and staying off the radar of investigators. Secretly however, He was living the high life and enjoying it to the fullest. Gonzalez stayed in only the finest hotels and lived like a rock star, celebrating his success extravagantly, traveling in style and driving a BMW 330i automobile, among other swanky purchases. He was reportedly so well off that, for one birthday, he threw himself a $75,000 party. In addition to this, he required a currency-counting machine just to be able to count out the daily profits of his hacks and even once complained of being annoyed when the machine broke, forcing him to count out hundreds of thousands of dollars by hand.

At the top of his game, Gonzalez could make over half a million dollars from hacking one company alone!

Fall from Grace: Eventually however, Alberto Gonzalez's good luck ran out. He was arrested in his room at the swanky National Hotel in Miami Beach, Florida in May of 2008. By 2009, he had officially been indicted on hacking charges that included the theft of 130 million card numbers as well as his role in his "Operation Get Rich or Die Tryin" scheme, an identity theft ring and many other offenses. Gonzalez ended up being sentenced to 20 years in prison for all of his hacks and ordered to forfeit millions of dollars in money and property.

Despite his eventual capture, Alberto Gonzalez's legacy lives on as a hacker who showed the leaders of gigantic corporations how a self-taught kid from Miami, Florida could easily become a multi-millionaire hacker and expose just how vulnerable both individuals and companies are to commonly used hacking techniques.

Kevin Mitnick: The Hacker King and Social Engineering Genius Who Changed the World

Born: 1963

Known Aliases: "The Condor" or "the Darkside Hacker"

When you talk about notorious hackers who changed the world, you can't fail to mention Kevin Mitnick.

Mitnick is without doubt the most famous hacker in the world, who as a young man notoriously broke into Nokia, Motorola, NEC and IBM's networks, among other famous corporations.

Hacker M.O.: Mitnick was raised in Los Angeles and during his adolescent years, had already begun his impressive career as a master of social engineering techniques. In fact, at only

13 years old, Mitnick was engaged in using social engineering to manipulate the Los Angeles bus system. He quickly figured out how to get past the punch card system by convincing a bus driver that he was doing a school project and needed to know where he could purchase a ticket punch like the ones used by the bus system employees. With his credible manner and his ease in talking to others, Mitnick managed to outwit the system and started to ride buses for free by making use of unused transfer slips that he'd "dumpster dived" for in the transport system's bus garage. In his career, this would be the hallmark of the so-called "hacker king"- psychologically manipulating unwitting targets into easily giving up what should have been highly confidential information.

At the young age of 16, Mitnick illegally hacked into a computer network for the first time. He did this by obtaining the telephone number for the computer system used by the Digital Equipment Corporation (DEC). Once in their system, Mitnick made illicit copies of DEC's software. For this crime, he received a 12 month prison stint but this was far from a deterrent to young Kevin. Instead, while still under supervised release, he figured out a method of hacking into Pacific Bell voice mail computers. This resulted in Mitnick being sought for these crimes and refusing to be captured, Mitnick fled, becoming a fugitive for several years.

During his years on the run, he never gave up on hacking, however. Instead, he worked out techniques that allowed him to illegally access tens of computer networks and even made copies of major cell phone and computer companies' software. He regularly read private emails and retrieved private information, including computer passwords. A master of deception, Mitnick was able to hide his location from investigators through the use of cloned cell phones and his long-standing skill at social engineering.

Man on the Run: Mitnick was chased in a highly publicized pursuit that eventually resulted in his arrest by the FBI in February of 1995. At the time of his capture and arrest, Mitnick's Raleigh, North Carolina apartment was found to be packed with over a hundred clone cell phone codes as well as forged identification materials and a whole host of cloned cell phones. His charges included 8 counts of possessing unauthorized access devices, 14 counts of committing wire fraud as well as unauthorized accessing of a federal computer, damaging said computer and intercepting electronic and wire communications.

There was a great deal of public interest in his case's court proceedings, which ended in Mitnick taking a plea deal. Mitnick served 5 years in prison which included an 8 month stint in solitary confinement. This strange measure was taken because judges actually believed Mitnick to be so dangerous that he could actually "start a nuclear war by whistling into a pay phone"!

In fact, Mitnick's main power lay in his extraordinary ability to psychological insights in order to manipulate almost anyone into giving him the information or access he desired. Later, Mitnick himself would go on to explain that a person could easily "hack" or enter and exploit phone and computer security, as he had done, without using any hacking tools, software programs.

Mitnick has always maintained that his primary and most powerful weapon in hacking has never been technology but his social engineering skills, as they were the main way he managed to retrieve passwords and code necessary for his hacks.

Continuing Fame: Unlike many so-called "dark" hackers, Kevin Mitnick was never really in it for the money. His interest lay in his fascination with all things related to computer systems and with understanding and using the workings of the human mind to his benefit. In fact, it is said that he never stole or illegally used a cent of money belonging to anyone else.

Still, that doesn't mean that he hasn't benefitted financially from his hacker knowledge. His amazing story has made him a recognized name and a celebrity both to the general public and to the citizens of the hacker underground. This fame has meant that 2 Hollywood movies have been made about his life and several books including those that he wrote himself have brought his story to a wider audience. In addition to the money brought in from that fame, Mitnick is also in high demand as a white hat hacker, offering his hacking skills to major corporations as a penetration tester and security consultant, uncovering the weaknesses that, at one time, he would have used himself to enter the systems of these companies. His white hat hacking firm, Mitnick Computer Security Consulting LLC has become such a resounding success with companies eager to protect themselves from hackers with skills like his, that he now has a net worth of at least $10,306,500.

Recently, Mitnick's company has also launched a new branch involved in the business of zero day exploit provision. Called "Mitnick's Absolute

Zero Day Exploit Exchange", this branch provides top government and corporate clients with advanced "zero-day exploits. These exclusive hacking tools will help Mitnick's clients to exploit unknown bugs in software. In the process of providing these exploits, Mitnick stands to make at least $100,000 per exploit sold.

This quickly adds up and despite not living a life of crime, Mitnick is well-placed to remain a multi-millionaire. His ability to go into legitimate business operations after being a known felon is yet another example of his amazing ability to gain the trust and confidence of others, using his knowledge of human nature.

Only Kevin Mitnick, the master of social engineering, could make the top companies he once targeted trust him enough to pay him millions of dollars for advice and security assistance!

These hackers and many that are at this very money, following in their footsteps have completely changed the world we live in. Their amazing abilities and shadowy exploits demonstrate that hacking is the key to the future and that it is only growing in power and influence. Understanding the motivations, minds and lives of hackers is just as important as understanding their skills and tricks, in order to truly protect yourself.

With that in mind, we'll be taking a close look at one of the most used tools and methods that malicious hackers use to pull off daring exploits that could be putting your device, information and privacy at risk right NOW! We'll also be following a step-by-step explanation that takes YOU inside the hack and uncovers all the details- Don't miss it!

Chapter 4:
Port Scanning Like A Professional Dark Web Hacker

A Hacker's Tool Belt: What is a Port Scanner?

A port scanner is a kind of software application that is utilized to search a host or server for the existence of any open ports. A port scan is comprised of numerous messages sent by whoever is trying to break into a device in order to ascertain what mind of network services are available on that device. Each of these services has its own identifiable port number. This application can be used in one of two ways.

It can be used for positive purposes by network administrators who want to find out just how secure their network's defenses are OR it can be used by your unfriendly neighborhood hacker in order to look for the services that are running on a host, seek out any weaknesses and vulnerabilities and use these in order to enter and exploit your network's security flaws. Port scanning is not intrinsically negative and is a very effective and useful way of auditing the robustness of your own network, if used properly. If, however, a port scanner falls into the wrong hands, you could be facing a hacker nightmare!

So how does a hacker use this tool against you?

Most malicious hackers love using port scanning as a technique because it allows them to assail your computer with a clearer idea of where their efforts should be aimed. When the hacker initiates a port scan, it essentially comprises of sending out a message to every port, kind of like knocking on many doors, one at a time.

When a response is received, the hacker can then see whether or not the port in question is being utilized on the device they are entering in and whether or not this port should be searched for vulnerabilities that will allow the hacker to enter the device.

Port scanning is carried out in two different ways: In the first method, the hacker scans one IP address in search of open ports. In the second method, the hacker scans a wide range of several IP addresses looking for open ports. A good way to understand port scanning is to compare it to calling numbers on the telephone. Seen from this perspective, the first method is similar to dialing one phone number and then seeking all of the possible extensions while the second method can be compared to calling a large range of numbers and then seeking every possible extension at each of the dialed numbers.

Two different protocols utilize ports. These are UDP and TCP. Both of these protocols have 65,536 individual ports. Internet services such as Web servers mainly listen on TCP port 80 while mail servers tend to listen on TCP door port 25.

When a hacker launches a port scan attack on your computer, they are sending packets to these different ports and the response they receive helps them to get an accurate idea of your device's security flaws. They are seeking to learn what your Operating System (OS) is like and to find a weaker spot to enter from. Many receive over a dozen port scans daily and unless your firewall is in great shape and you ensure that the services allowed to pass through it are limited, you could be facing a big problem.

Here's a step-by-step rundown of how a hacker can maliciously use port scanning to break into your device. While a black hat hacker ca do this to steal your information, take over your device and generally mess with your life, you don't have to use these steps in a negative manner. In fact, if you use these steps to try to test your own security, you can easily find and fix your weak spots before a hacker beats you to it!

STEPS FOR PERFORMING A SUCCESSFUL PORT SCAN LIKE A PRO HACKER

1. The hacker initiates the port scanning. The port scanner then sends TCP SYN requests in order to scan the host or hosts the hacker has selected for scanning.

2. Because most scanners only scan TCP ports by default, a skilled hacker will make sure to scan UDP ports by using a dedicated UDP port scanner, in order not to miss a thing. (**Insider Hacker Tip**: If you're looking for an effective UDP port scanner, Nmap and SuperScan are both very good choices!)

3. The port scanner then awaits responses from hosts.

4. The port scanner searches all of the hosts, looking through 65, 535 TCP and UDP ports, seeking those with available services. This tells the hacker which services are available.

5. BINGO! Now the hacker knows the following very useful information: Which hosts are active and can be reached via the network, the addresses of these active hosts and which applications or services are available on these hosts.

6. The hacker can now look deeper into the specifics of targeted hosts discovered.

Many people choose SuperScan for their basic TCP port scan needs. When using this port scanning tool, you can either choose to have the tool scan only the responsive pings and selected listed ports or you can also add the following steps on:

- If you want your scan test to be more precise and accurate, you can block ICMP.

- You may be interested in scanning only a specific range of ports and SuperScan can allow you to do so. In order to achieve this, select the option called ALL Selected Ports in List. Make sure that you scan all 65, 535 for the first time.

Nmap is a much more advanced sport scanning tool and will yield you more detailed and focused results. It will scan ports in such a way as to ascertain which ports are really open and available so it helps to eliminate closed ports showing up as though they were open. With Nmap, you can also do a UDP scan, (as I mentioned above) to find any open UDP ports and to ascertain which applications or services are running on these scanned hosts. This will also help you to find out whether the connections are being logged by firewalls or other devices.

You can also use Nmap for a standard TCP scan to seek out open ports, find out what's running on the host and whether connections are being logged.

Do a SYN Stealth scan to look for and try out loggers like firewalls etc.

If you apply scans such as Null, FIN Stealth and Xmas Tree, they will test out hosts and show up any weaknesses that need attention, where possible entry could become an issue.

WARNING!!! How NOT to Crash the System You are Scanning!

There have been many cases of people performing port scanning who have ended up crashing their whole system or applications within it. I'm not including this here to scare you or dissuade you but rather to inform you, as that's the main purpose of this book. That's why

I've included the following tips to help you ensure that what started as a simple trial port scan doesn't end up as a disaster for your system or the system you are scanning.

If you are not careful when doing these port scans, you could actually end up launching a Denial of Service on your own system or the system you're scanning and bringing it down. Make sure that you don't do this type of port scanning activity if the software that is in charge of the TCP/IP on the host you are scanning is not strong. That's because a weak TCP/IP stack can easily lead to a Denial of Service problem.

In order to make this risk much less likely to occur, make sure that you choose the slower timing choices offered by Nmap. These are Polite, Paranoid or Sneaky and these options are your best bet to avoid major DoS complications. Keeping these tips in mind will help you to avert issues with crashing systems and applications and will make your port scanning activity a success.

Types of Port Scans Used include:

A Vanilla Port Scan: This is when a port scan tries to connect to all 65,536 possible ports.

A Stealth Scan: This is a sly way of scanning. It's when scanning methods are used that try to keep the request from being logged by firewalls and other logging devices.

A Strobe Scan: This is when a port scan tries to only connect with a few targeted ports, usually less than 20 chosen ports.

A Sweep Scan: This is a type of port scan done on the same selected port but carried out across several computers.

A UDP Scan: This type of port scan specifically scans for UDP ports, which are User Datagram Protocol ports.

A Fragmented Packets Scan: This scan type involves sending out fragmented packets in order to allow them to bypass the packet filters that firewalls have.

A FTP Bounce Scan: This type of port scan is very popular with malicious hackers because it involves hiding the hacker's location by directing the attempts through an FTP (File Transfer Protocol) server.

So now that you have all the background information on port scans and a step-by-step showing how professional malicious hackers carry out these port scans, wouldn't you like to know more about the ways hackers use port scanning for their own benefit? Without further ado, here's the story of master port scanner Max Bulter. This clearly illustrates just how lucrative and essential port scanning is for all the black hat hackers who need to find a way in before they can begin exploiting.

Max "the Iceman" Bulter and the Aloha Port Scanning Hack

Max Bulter, now known as Max Ray Vision (formerly Max Ray Butler, AKA the Iceman) was once a computer security consultant from Meridian, Idaho who is currently serving a 13 year prison sentence for hacking. His sentence is the longest ever handed down in history for hacking in the United States of America. In his brief hacking career, Bulter managed to steal almost 2 million credit card numbers and racked up fraudulent charges of nearly $90 million. And what was his favorite hacking move? You guessed it, port scanning!

Bulter was considered a gray hat hacker because he often offered his services to organizations and even law enforcement to find and patch up weaknesses in other's systems. However, he also went on to develop the famed arachNIDS(reference archive of current heuristics for network intrusion detection systems) database and ended up finding out that the Aloha Point-of-Sale (POS) system had a remote backdoor in their systems that was installed for the purpose of providing technical help to clients. Because many smaller restaurants use Aloha systems, Max Bulter knew that this would potentially give him access to thousands of credit card numbers.

With this knowledge in hand, Bulter set up a U.S-wide scanning program in order to continually scan for any system with an open port 5505. Because port 5505 is not utilized by other services, this would immediately throw up a flag letting Bulter know that the computer in question was running Aloha's system and that there was an available vulnerability to exploit.

Every time Bulter found this port open, he would launch an exploit against the open port and service, seeking out and retrieving large amounts of credit card numbers. Because he founded the infamous Carders market, a forum for black hat hackers to trade, buy and sell credit card numbers and other sensitive information from each other, Bulter was able to sell each of these credit card numbers retrieved through the port scanning hack for up to $50 a piece. In this way, he was able to make over $86 million dollars in a short space of time.

Ultimately, Bulter's success was enormous but also short lived. He ended up being caught and incarcerated in a low-security prison, ordered to pay out over $20 million of restitution money to the victims and will only be released in 2019. Still, his exploits have made port scanning known for being one of the fastest and easiest ways to make millions overnight and the simplicity of the steps above show just how anyone with a computer, the ability to type on a keyboard and lack of moral hang-ups is able to become a multi-millionaire malicious hacker in no time!

Chapter 5:
The Web's Dangerous Side - Trojan Horses: The Threat Disguised as a Gift

No guide on navigating the world of hacking secrets would ever be complete without delving into the subject of Trojans. Not knowing about Trojans is the internet equivalent of going into battle blind. That's why I've chosen to create an entire chapter on this important topic. Let's start with the name:

"Trojan" refers to the ancient Greek tale of the battle against the city of Troy. After spending 10 years fighting the citizens of Troy in vain, the Greeks finally came up with a very cunning way to win the war. They constructed an enormous wooden horse and placed a select group of their soldiers inside it. They then proceeded to present this horse at the gates of the city of Troy and pretended to leave. The citizens of Troy looked out and seeing this wooden horse, believed it was a gift of surrender from the Greeks. They opened their gates and pulled the horse into their city, not realizing that there were enemy soldiers inside it. The Greeks were then able to take advantage of this opportunity to enter the fortified city and destroy it.

So why do we refer to modern-day malicious computer malware as Trojans today? Well, the simple answer is that just as the Greeks disguised a threat in the form of a gift and tricked the unsuspecting citizens of Troy into accepting it, modern-day computer hackers use innocuous, innocent or even beneficial seeming disguises to trick you into clicking on, opening and activating their dangerous Trojan malware.

Trojans are frequently disguised in the form of legitimate, safe and useful software, including popular program downloads. When hackers send a Trojan to you, they know that as long as they present it in a manner that makes you believe it to be harmless, they have an excellent shot at getting into your computer, controlling your system and harvesting enormous amounts of private and valuable information.

What are the Main Characteristics of a Trojan Horse?

- Trojan horses are not able to self-replicate automatically

- Trojan horses are often sent in the guise of a harmless or useful program or download

- Trojan horses make your system vulnerable to further harm

How a Trojan Horse Can Affect Your Device

Trojan horses are able to go virtually undetected and can be used in a variety of ways, making them a favorite of unethical hackers.

When a Trojan is activated, it can:

- Allow hackers to watch your every move

- Allow hackers to steal and delete your valuable data

- Allow hackers to disrupt the way your computer or network works by crating backdoors that enable them to take charge of your device

- Allow hackers to change or make copies of your vital information

When hackers send a Trojan horse to you, their main aims include exploring your device and gaining access to private, sensitive data such as your user identification and your computer and account passwords. Advanced hackers will also send more highly developed Trojan horses in order to specifically look for and retrieve targeted information such as your credit card information or your bank account data. Such hackers will then do far more than simply control your system. They'll take this hacking attack into the real world, by using this sensitive data to usurp your identity, empty your bank accounts, make illicit charges to your credit cards and even commit crimes in your name. When such sophisticated methods are used against your computer, a skilled hacker can then takeover your computer-essentially forcing it to be part of a network that targets and harms other user's computers.

Important!!! If You Have an Apple Device, You Are Not Necessarily Safe From a Trojan Infection!

I hear it all the time. Apple device owners believe they are using devices that are by design, completely immune to being infected by a Trojan. After all, Mac OS X is just about infection-proof, right? Well, not anymore. Enter the Flashback Trojan. While for many years, Apple users could rest easy about potential threats from viruses, worms and hackers, those days are unfortunately, long gone. In fact, the Flashback Trojan that first began to be detected in 2011 is now one of the major Trojan threats around. As the most serious security risk to Macs around the world, Flashback Trojans have infected well over 700,000 Macs and MacBooks on the OS X platform and the infections are only growing.

This Trojan type affects your Mac device by seeking out and taking advantage of Mac OS X vulnerabilities. What happens is that you, as a use, are forcibly redirected to a false site. Here an application is loaded through the use of JavaScript Code and an executable file is then allowed to save itself to your computer. Your device is now open to the downloading and running of malicious code. At this point, the hacker who set up this Trojan trap for you now has complete control of your device.

So what can you do to identify a Trojan infection on your Mac or MacBook?

You can easily find out if your device has a Trojan problem by running a trio of commands.

Go to Terminal, which is located in Utilities, in your Mac's Application folder. Then, copy and paste the following code strings into Terminal.

defaults read /Applications/Safari.app/Contents/Info LSEnvironment

defaults read /Applications/Firefox.app/Contents/Info LSEnvironment

defaults read ~/.MacOSX/environment DYLD_INSERT_LIBRARIES

These commands will inform you that these domain/default pairs do not exist, if your device is free from a Trojan infection. However, if your device does have a Trojan problem, these commands will show the patch in which the malware was installed into your device.

The best way to deal with any infections you do find is to use a specific third-party tool from Norton or other companies to remove any Trojans discovered.

Trojans on Your Phone: Did you know that Trojans can infect your smartphone as well as your other devices? Once a Trojan has been activated on your smartphone, hackers can then get it to send expensive SMS messages to high-cost premium phone numbers. These hackers then collect the money you are unwittingly spending on these messages.

Trojans horses fall into different classifications based on how they behave once activated on your computer:

Exploits: Exploit Trojans are programs with code that enables them to make use of inherent security weaknesses within software that is running on your device.

Backdoors: Backdoor Trojans hand over control of your device to hackers. Once activated, backdoors allow the malicious controller to basically OWN your device.. The hacker becomes able to delete, send or receive files, reboot your device and carry out almost any other command under the sun. When hackers want to use your computer as part of a "slave chain" or network of devices that are used to harm other devices or carry out other illegal activities, they tend to use backdoors.

Rootkits: Rootkit Trojans are created to be able to hide activities within your system. They the ultimate Trojan within a Trojan, because their disguise allows them to conceal the existence of newly activated malicious programs. This in turn allows them to keep you from seeing and dealing with the Trojan infection on your device until it is too late!

Trojan-DDoS: Trojan DdoS programs carry out DoS (Short for Denial of Service) campaigns against a specific address. This program works by using a ring of infected computers such as your own to send numerous requests to a specific web address. This leads to the address being unable to cope with so many requests and eventually results in a (DoS) denial of service.

Trojan-Dropper: A Trojan-Dropper is a program that hackers employ in Trojan installation and it's also used to help stop malicious programs from being found. Because many different types of popular antivirus programs are not able to go through and detect the various components of a Trojan-Dropper, it's an extremely effective tool for hackers who want to get in AND stay in your device, uninterrupted.

Trojan-Downloader: This type of Trojan is able to download various new and updated versions of Trojans onto your computer.

Trojan-GameThief: This type of Trojan program uses the gaming world to accumulate important private data by stealing account information from those who participate in online gaming.

Trojan-IM: These types of Trojan programs utilize methods that allow it to swipe your instant messaging account passwords and login details. Instant messaging programs like MSN Messenger and Skype are particularly vulnerable to this Trojan.

Trojan-Mailfinder: This program type enables hacker to retrieve email addresses from your computer's address book.

Trojan-FakeAV: Trojan-FakeAV programs simulate the activity of antivirus software. They are designed to extort money from you – in return for the detection and removal of threats... even though the threats that they report are actually non-existent.

Trojan-SMS: As mentioned above, these types of Trojan programs are designed to siphon off our money by forcing your infected smartphone to send expensive texts to premium numbers.

Trojan-Spy: Trojan-Spy programs allow hackers to watch every move you make on your device through a variety of methods that include capturing screen shots, tracking your keyboard and your applications.

Trojan-Clicker: Trojan-Clickers are programs that install themselves onto your device and try to send themselves to other devices. Ironically, these programs are often disguised as spyware removal programs, enticing users to click on them and silently wreaking havoc on infected systems.

Trojan-Ransom: Trojan-Ransom programs install themselves on your device and then change the data on your device to make it impossible for your device to work properly. You'll know a Trojan-Ransom infection has taken place because you'll receive a ransom message from the hacker, letting you know that you'll have to pay the ransom amount they require, in order to access your data or have your device returned to normal running.

Other Trojan Program Types Are:

- Trojan-Proxy

- Trojan-Notifier

- Trojan-PSW

What Are the Immediate and Long Term Effects of a Trojan Infection on Your Device?

- It can lead to a drastically slowed down connection.

- It can slow down your computer or even lead to a complete computer crash.

- It can prevent your computer from starting up or shutting down properly by activating processes continually.

- It can cause the display of non-stop error messages on your computer.

- It can basically takeover your browser and force you to be redirected to the sites IT wants you to go to, keeping you away from the sites YOU want to visit.

- It can allow criminal hackers to collect your private information from your computer and could lead to you having your identity stolen.

- It can use your computer to spread illicit files and launch infections into other devices.

- It can allow hackers to control your system, connection and all other resources.

- It can allow hackers to send out emails from your account that you know nothing about. These emails could be offensive or illicit and lead to a loss of reputation for you or your business/company.

- It can lead to the appearance of unrecognizable or unfamiliar desktop icons.

- It can allow spam to overwhelm your inbox and the inboxes of your email contacts.

- It can cause the appearance of toolbars you don't recognize or normally use.

The Trojan Hack:

Alright, now that we've looked at the background information on Trojan infections, it's time to delve into one of the most popular hacks that cyber-criminals pull on unsuspecting victims, using the very common but equally dangerous Trojan Horse programs. **Please note:** I am including this information into this book because ignoring the issue of Trojan hacks will not make the problem go away and would lead to all kinds of serious repercussions for your devices and for your life as a whole. With that in mind, let's take a look at how hackers "gift" you a very dangerous Trojan infection, all wrapped up to look like a pleasant present and how they social engineer you into innocently accepting this unsavory delivery. We call this:

The Trojan Hack

Trojan Hack # 1:

This is by far the most common and widespread method of Trojan delivery used by cyber-criminals today. Here's how it goes:

Hacker Goal: With this hack, the hacker's goal is to make you install the Trojan server onto your device's system. In order to achieve this, the hacker will first send you an email containing the server file (let's call it "anything".exe, because .exe denotes any executable file). Usually the email will have an interesting and safe or reassuring sounding subject line and very often, it will have been sent to you via a friend (who has probably unknowingly been infected with a Trojan and is not behind the email in the first place). This makes it very easy for you to trust the email and click on the file it contains. What happens next is the important part- NOTHING! That's right, no file opening, no game starting, just nothing. But how can a non-event be so threatening, you may ask?

Well, the answer to that is that while you see nothing happening on your screen's display, something very nefarious and underhanded is happening within your device's system. While you're impatiently clicking and re-clicking away, the hacker has now installed the Trojan server onto your device's system and you never noticed a thing! Now, the hacker can simply connect to your system by employing the Trojan Client.

At this point, the doors of your once private system swing wide open and the hacker is able to step inside. You are no longer in the driver's seat because the hacker now has access to absolutely every part of your system. Congratulations! Clicking on an unknown file has led you to being "Owned".

Now, be honest with yourself, haven't you done this before? The fact is that we've all received an email from someone we know and ended up clicking open a file that seemed to do nothing. It's a rookie mistake and one that millions of people have made, which is why hacker's love this method of hacking so much it gives them quick and easy access to the every move of people across the world, without them having to really lift a finger. But on the flip side, this hack is also a victim of its own success, which is to say that now, millions of formerly innocent victims are not so innocent anymore. Many have become aware that clicking on a file that apparently does nothing is a sure sign that a Trojan has been installed. Therefore, they rush to remove this Trojan before it can allow hackers to enter their accounts and harvest their private data.

For hackers, this is clearly not good. They've essentially lost the element of surprise and the stealth of their move. This has led them to develop a more sophisticated, less obvious hacking technique for Trojan delivery. Here's how it goes:

Trojan Hack # 2:

Hackers have managed to figure out how to use programs that allow them to put a real .exe (executable) file together with a Trojan server file. This joining makes a nasty combination which will look very similar to a legitimate .exe file of some type. For instance, a hacker may take a legitimate game file like a Sudoku puzzle .exe file and combine it with a malicious Trojan server to produce a tainted file that they will now send to you. The hacker will name this tainted file something harmless, such as sudokupuzzle.exe and send it off to you and thousands of other potential victims. What happens next? You receive this file (again, probably through an infected friend or acquaintances account) and click on the Sudoku puzzle game.

Here's the really tricky part of the hack: The game actually opens normally. You begin enjoying your new Sudoku puzzle that someone has thoughtfully sent to you while underneath the surface, all havoc is breaking loose. The Trojan has now been installed onto your system! The next awful step in this chain of events is that while you're happily going about business as usual on you device, the Trojan has made a home in your system and now sends out a message to the hacker who sent it. This message typically will contain private information about you including your IP address (making you instantly locatable to any hacker who wants to find you) a username, and your online status (this alerts your hacker every time you get on the internet). So as you can see, the method may be slightly different but the net result is the same-your system and device are owned again.

What's worse is that with this more sophisticated trick, you don't even have the chance to become suspicious because the game or whatever file you were sent opened and ran properly. You have nothing to alert you to the fact that a Trojan was installed on your device's system. As a result, you're not even thinking about the possible need to do a removal. All the hacker has to do now is sit back and control your device, ransacking your data for important information that could potentially lead to your money and identity being stolen, your device being used against other devices as part of an illicit network or your colleagues and friends receiving false and embarrassing emails and posts from "your" account.

The good news is that you now know about how a hacker carries out these Trojan hacks, making you better placed to put a stop to this kind of infection before it can happen to you.

One last thought that I want to leave you with in this section is simply this- just because you received an attachment from someone you know doesn't mean that it's a good idea to just open it. Many of us put a lot of trust in the grapevine or network of friends we have online but sometimes, that grapevine may be poisoned. Beware!

Make sure to join me in the next section where I'll be showing you which files are safe to open and which ones you need to delete right away! Trust me, this information could save your device and prevent a lot of pain, embarrassment and trouble for you. You DON'T want to miss it!

Chapter 6:
Safe VS Unsafe Files - A Look Inside the Hacker's Bag of Tricks, Part 1

So you may now be questioning if all files arc basically out of bounds for you and feeling that it's too unsafe to open any type of file from now on. While there are definitely risks involved in receiving and opening files there's absolutely no reason to give in to fear or paranoia.

In this section I will be showing you the very best ways to ensure that you stay safe while opening files you've received. The trick to outsmarting those sneaky hackers is to stay one step ahead at all times by understanding the hacker mentality. Malicious hackers who want to enter your device and steal your information are generally looking for the easy way in. Therefore, they'll use some pretty simple techniques which are made hard to resist through social engineering, but if you know what to look for, you'll be able to block these attempts.

The easiest way to infect someone's computer is to send them a false executable file (an .exe file) which will then install a Trojan into your system once you've double clicked on it. This is why the first step in warding off a Trojan hack is to keep an eagle-eye watch on files that could potentially fall into this category.

Never, under any circumstances, should you ignore the extensions at the end of all file names, as this is your biggest clue to the origins and legitimacy of any file you receive. Here, we will be focusing on safe and unsafe files-how to recognize them, how to deal with them and what to look out for. With this knowledge under your belt, you'll be able to fend off even the sneakiest Trojan hack campaigns that a malicious hacker can throw at your device.

Let's take a look at document files first:

Appropriate Formats for Text and Read Me Files:

The vast majority of all documents often have these formats and they are basically documents created in a word processing program. These kinds of program information documents usually have the following types of extensions at the end of their file names:

TXT (Such as "blank".txt) - This kind of file is openable in Microsoft Word, Notepad etc.

Doc (Such as "blank".doc)-This document format can e opened by Word or Microsoft Word.

RTF (Such as "blank". rtf)

These formats above are usually the safe and appropriate formats for Text and Read Me files to come in, but if a text file comes in the following formats, you know there's a problem.

Formats that Point to a Suspicious Text and Read Me:

.exe

.txt.vbs

.com

If a text document bears any of these extensions at the end of its file name-AVOID IT LIKE THE PLAGUE!!!

What about images? Well, just like text documents, pictures come in a pretty set list of format types and anytime you receive a picture bearing an extension that is not on this list, you should be very careful about opening it.

In particular, hackers will often try to send you a picture in the .exe file (executable file) format. Whatever the reason they give you for doing so, never accept or open this file type for pictures. Simply trash the file right away and report it to your email server as soon as possible!

So what are the appropriate formats for pictures? It can vary but these are the most frequently used types and they are the only ones that I can recommend as an image file type you can comfortably open:

- TIFF (Such as "blank".tiff)

- JPG (Such as "blank".jpg)

- GIF (Such as "blank".gif)

- BMP (Such as "blank".bmp)

Only trust these extensions on your picture files and steer clear of an executable (.exe) file ending, in order to ensure that your computer is a whole lot safer from possible Trojan infections in the future!

Can Audio and Video File Contain a Trojan?

While audio and video files are not commonly considered to potentially be malicious or infected file types, they are increasingly being infected by malicious hackers as an unusual and therefore, unexpected way to infect devices and enter systems. More and more, we see malware embedded in video files or even masquerading as video files.

These are some of the most common reasons for infection to exist in video files:

Because media players are highly used, they are often left open for long periods of time and while users are carrying out other tasks, making them a perfect Trojan hotspot.

- While everyone is highly aware of the risks posed by infected documents and images, very few people view media files as potential sources of Trojan infection, making them a hacker's dream method of getting into your device. If someone passes you a media file, you are much more likely to play it than you would be if someone sent you a document or image file to open.

- There are many different kinds of audio players, file plugins and codecs and these are not created by those with a strong security focus.

- Media players often take insecure input from various sources that are not verified. There are also cases in which lower privilege IE instances can place content into high privilege Windows Media Player.

  How many times have you visited a web page and noticed that a media file of some type was already embedded into that page? This makes them an easy method of passing Trojans to unsuspecting victims.

The usual weaknesses we find in media files are media player fuzzing and hyperlinks embedded into a video file. While fuzzing is a problem, it is much trickier to successfully carry out so hackers tend to choose the hyperlink embedding route instead. When the appropriate URL is embedded into a modern media file, it opens the door for hackers to get their Trojans in.

One example of this would be in the Microsoft ASF which is open to the execution of simple script commands. When the code executes, the unsuspecting victim receives notification to download for the ability to play the video or audio file. This routes the victim to a site that is indeed malicious and will lead to a Trojan infection.

Prior warning makes for better protection so here is a list of the most popular media file formats that hackers love to exploit in order to re-route users:

- Adobe Flash.swf

- Real Media

- .rmvb

- Real Media

- .rm/.rmvb

- Windows

- .wma/.wmv

- QucikTime.mov

- Windows.asf

Ways to Avoid Trojan Infection from Dubious Media Files:

Everything from the exploitation of digital rights management flaws to the launching or malicious pages and the infection of .asf files for the purpose of embedding links to malicious pages has been detected in these popular media files so never take an audio or video file at face value again. Instead, try to be as sure of the source, creator and distributor as possible before clicking play. Also, make sure that you aren't running a media player that has high privileges and always refuse unfamiliar codec downloads.

Chapter 7:
Social Engineering-The Greatest Hack of Them All - A Look Inside the Hacker's Bag of Tricks, Part 2

While you could be forgiven for believing that hackers primarily work with technological devices, the truth is that the most important and complex piece of equipment that cyber-criminals could ever "hack" into is the human mind. When malicious hackers use non-technical tactics to gain the trust, faith and acceptance of their victims, this is called social engineering and it is the single greatest threat to your security today.

Social engineering works so well because of its non-technical nature. Simply put, human beings are social creatures and we have a tendency to want to believe and relate to other human beings. As such, it is far easier to bypass human disbelief and suspicion, using a winning, confident manner and highly polished lies than it is to bypass the security protocols of devices using coding and other hacking tools. Even when a hacker employs a social engineering hack not involving direct human contact, he or she still uses their understanding of human nature to craft a perfect scam that victims easily fall for.

Criminals have been using social methods to enter the wallets, homes and lives of their victims for thousands of years and the only real difference when it comes to the social engineering techniques used by hackers today is its online component.

The problem is growing exponentially and has become truly alarming, with global hackers setting up entire fake "call centers" staffed by professional criminal hackers who pretend to be "customer service agents" and talk their way into receiving the sensitive financial and personal information that you normally would never even consider giving away.

Social engineering is big business and the hackers who are really running the dark web are concentrating on it more and more as their favorite business model. So what's the upshot of all of this for you? You need to become very aware of social engineering tricks that these hacker criminals are using to make sure that they never use them against you successfully. That is the only real way to prevent a cyber-criminal from getting his or her hands on your money, your secrets, your life and even the safety and security of yourself and your loved ones.

This is why I've dedicated a chapter to this topic and included all of the information you NEED to know today, to keep yourself from ever falling for a sophisticated social engineering hacking campaign, before it's too late!

Before we delve into all of the details, let's first take a look at the meaning of social engineering.

When we refer to social engineering within the context of hacking, we are talking about highly planned psychological manipulation of hacking targets in order to get them to either make a certain desired move or to give the hacker private information.

At its core, it is very similar to the classic "con" because of its human element, but unlike a mere confidence trick, social engineering often combines human hacking with technological methods to create a scam that is incredibly hard to resist or prevent. Also, unlike many of the common frauds out there, social engineering involves many detailed and intricate steps that require a great deal of patience and skill but that when successful, can inflict serious harm on the individual targeted for hacking.

In order to carry out social engineering, criminal hackers will use their knowledge of collective "cognitive biases". A cognitive bias, when looked at from a tech point of view, is similar to a flaw in our hardware. It is an inherent error in human thinking that causes us to make less-than-great decisions and is a weakness that hackers can identify and easily exploit for their purposes. A good example of a cognitive bias would be the "probability neglect". This is the cognitive bias that makes us believe that one thing is less dangerous than another, even if the second thing has actually been proven to be equally or even more risky.

Hackers exploit this vulnerability when they make expedition phone calls, seeking sensitive information from the person on the other end of the line. The person may be unlikely to give away this information to someone who emails them but will end up giving that same information to a caller, thinking that email scams are somehow more of a threat than phone calls. The reality is that there are a large number of phone scams and that giving your information to a caller is no less dangerous than giving it to someone who emails you for it-both are risky, but the hacker knows that people's cognitive biases will lead them astray and help the hacker to achieve his or her goal.

Now that you see how hackers employ cognitive bias flaws in the same way that they exploit glitches or bugs in hardware, let's look at the different methods that hackers use in order to successfully social engineer their targets.

Any social engineering hack generally falls into one of two categories: Human-driven and computer-driven. While human-driven social engineering hacks utilize person-to-person contact to obtain confidential information, computer-driven social engineering hacks involve the use of computer software in order to gain confidential information

First, let's examine human-driven hacks.

Human-Driven Social Engineering Hacks Include:

The Official Impersonation Hack: This is an extremely popular human-driven social engineering hack that involves the hacker gaining private information by actually impersonating an employee or other valid user to enter a closed area. Tall the hacker needs for this hack is a convincing uniform, a confident natural manner and perhaps a few props. In this way, many hackers have pretended to be delivery men, company employees or other authorized personnel. This allows them to gain physical access to a system and if they're quick and skilled about it, to retrieve the information they seek. Hackers also use the impersonation technique to telephone a company's desktop support line, pretending to be an employee and to use this method of accessing information. The hacker doesn't even necessarily need to do much for this social engineering technique to yield unbelievable results.

The Notice Board Hack: This hack falls under the same impersonation category, but is so easy that almost anyone can pull it off, with very little risk. Imagine that a person walks into a crowded company during a very busy day, would anyone much attention? The fact is that most people wouldn't. And if that same person happened to quickly put up a notice on the company notice board, with an official heading, announcing that the company help desk's number had changed and supplying a new number, most people wouldn't catch that either.

This is a method that hackers are using more frequently because they can just post the notice and slip out and wait for their phone to start ringing with help desk requests from the target company's employees. The hacker can then plausibly ask for the employees' name, company ID number and eve address and date of birth,-for "verification" purposes. The hacker will then use this goldmine of information to either target each employee specifically or the company as a whole for a lucrative hack.

The Dumpster Diving Hack: This move involves hackers searching the trash of a company or individual to find important bits of information. For example, a person may easily throw away a bank statement including their name, address and telephone number. A hacker who finds this has hit pay dirt because he or she can now telephone their victim fully equipped with enough information about the victim to appear to be from the victim's bank. In this way, the hacker can receive information like PINs, account numbers and even Social

Security numbers-all from a bit of digging in the trash!

When it comes to companies, a hacker can find filenames, company passwords and even detailed financial information about the company's clientele in the trash. I'm sure you can imagine just how damaging this can end up being.

The Phone Phishing Hack: In this human-driven social engineering hack, the hacker simply puts on their best phone manner and calls the target up, pretending to be from a trust-worthy institution, for example, a health insurance company. If it is a targeted hack, meaning that the hacker has already gathered some preliminary information on the victim, the hacker will know the target's name and the name of his or her health insurer.

Once the target hears the hacker's assured and official-sounding introduction, he or she will be very likely to believe the story that the call is from his or her health insurance company and that it is a request for verification of identity because "someone may have gotten medical attention under his or her name".

The hacker will use some very reliable social engineering tricks, such as empathy, telling the victim that he or she completely understands how stressful this news must be and that the company is ready to do everything possible to help the victim combat whoever is impersonating them. Reassured by the official manner of the hacker and the empathy he or she is receiving, the victim will probably give the caller whatever information is requested-even if it is highly sensitive or confidential. This kind of hack is a classic example of pretexting. Pretexting is a social engineering technique that hackers often use to establish trust. They do this by learning enough about the victim beforehand to create a very believable pretext for contacting them or engaging them in conversation.

Now let's get into the second category of social engineering hacks, computer-driven social engineering:

Computer-Driven Social Engineering Hacks Include:

The Email Phishing Hack: Phishing refers to a social engineering method used by hackers to gain what should be confidential information from unwitting victims. Phishing works in this way: the hacker sends an official-looking email to the target, purporting to be from the a legitimate institution that the target trusts, such as the target's credit card company, bank or even doctor's office. In this email, the hacker cleverly asks the target to verify his or her identity because some "criminal activity" appears to have been carried out under the target's name. If it's a bank, the target will immediately believe that someone has been taking his or her money illegally and if it's a doctor's office, he or she will believe that someone has perhaps gotten a hold of his or her Social Security number and is gaining medical care through it.

Because the target believes in the legitimacy of the email AND fears the information provided to him or her, he or she will be likely to comply with the email's instructions immediately. Hackers often include a link within the email that will redirect the victim to an equally legitimate-looking web page where he or she will be asked to enter private information such as name, address, date of birth, credit card number or even Social Security number.

If a hacker is truly daring he or she may even ask you to fill in your ATM card's PIN! Now, it may seem like a trap that only the most ignorant or innocent person would fall into, but the truth is, with millions of victims and counting, phishing really does work. One example of a popular phishing scam used by hackers in recent times is the "update account information" hack. The hacker would send the victim an email that appeared to be from a major and well-known online retailer. The email would explain that if the target didn't update his or her account information right away, the retailer would have to immediately suspend the target's account. Well, you might ask- how would the hackers know if their targets actually had accounts with that retailer? The answer is two-fold: If it is a targeted social engineering hack, the hacker has probably been following their target's movements online for a while and via malware, may have seen the sites visited by the target. This would mean that the hacker would have a pretty good idea of whether or not the target had an account with the retailer. Another option would be that the hack was a random one and that the hacker is simply sending out thousands of emails to many different people, looking for one to "bite". Because the retailer that the hacker is impersonating is a major one, chances are high that at least a certain percentage of people who receive the email will indeed have an account with that retailer and will be likely to believe the message.

The IVR Hack: Sometimes the email message will include instructions to call the "retailer" at a specifically created toll-free telephone number for secure verification. When the target calls this number they will be routed to a "vishing" line, where a fraudulent IVR (interactive voice response) system has been designed to mimic the retailer's real IVR system.

This automated voice response system will prompt the target to enter log-in details and then repeatedly tell them that log-in has failed. This way the target will enter and re-enter passwords over and over, and will even try other passwords. The end result is that the hacker will wind up with many of the target's passwords and log-in details and can now hack many of the target's different accounts with this information, instead of just one.

The Online Scam Hack: This social engineering hack can involve hooking a target via a pop-up window advertising a desirable and legitimate looking program download that appears to come from the company making the program, which is actually a piece of malicious software in disguise. It can also involve sending a target a malicious attachment in the form of a friendly, interesting or urgent email message.

Once opened, these attachments will typically unleash malicious code encompassing everything from key loggers that will log the user's every stroke and save his or her account passwords, username and other important details to Trojan infections that will pass over complete control of the target's device to the hacker, allowing the hacker to access any data within the device.

The Baiting Hack: This social engineering method is based on appealing to human nature's curious side. A hacker will attempt to bait their target by tempting them with something that will either satisfy their curiosity or pique their interest such as peer-to-peer torrent download of a copyrighted material. Some hackers even leave an enticingly labelled USB flash drive in an area where their target is sure to find it and then just sit back and wait for curiosity to do the rest. In fact, many an employee has infected their company's devices and systems by finding a USB flash drive labelled "Approved Promotions and Raises" or something like that, in the company restrooms and plugging it into their device.

The targeted employee believes that the USB drive must have been accidentally left behind and is perfectly safe (and interesting to view) but the truth is that a hacker installed malicious software on that USB, labelled it to catch someone's eye and strategically "left" it somewhere where the target would find it. Human beings will always take a peek when they know they're not supposed to and this leads to security vulnerabilities.

Again, here's a case of hackers understanding the human psyche so well that they can manipulate and crack it as though it were an easy-to-hack system.

How to Perform a Professional Social Engineering Hack:

Alright, now that we've gone over some of the most important and popular social engineering hack techniques, let's get down to the specifics:

I'm going to show you how to perform several powerful social engineering hacks that leave targets' information squarely in your hands.

Disclaimer: IMPORTANT!!!

Please note that I put together a few important hacking tutorials within this chapter in order to highlight how hackers combine their knowledge of human flaws and foibles and their in-depth tech hacking skills into a dangerous concoction that can seriously affect your life. These hacking tutorials are included here purely as a means of showing how almost anyone can easily trick you into believing them and allowing them to have risky access to your device, network, personal details, your list of friends and work contacts and so much more! These tutorials are meant to familiarize you with the secret techniques used by social engineering hackers to find you, obtain background information about you and gain unauthorized entry into your machine and your private life.

Please use these tutorials as an opportunity to try these techniques out on your own computer, to test its security or to test the availability of information about you on social media sites and other places online that could leave you vulnerable to a real-life malicious hack. Please also keep in mind that many types of social engineering hacks are illegal and could end up causing unwanted consequences if tried out on anyone without their permission. With this in mind, check out these steps and good luck and happy ethical hacking!

Social Engineering Hack #1: How to Perform the "Job Offer" Hack

- 1st, let's name our imaginary target "Mr. John Doe". Theoretically, you would head to Google and type "Mr. John Doe" into the search bar.

- This basic Google search should turn up everything from John Doe's Twitter handle and Facebook page to his LinkedIn profile and blogs. Among these pages you can see what John Doe looks like, where he went to school, what his profession is, where he lives and his entire network of friends and colleagues etc. If you're a good observer, you can even gather hints about the target's personality and the best way to approach him. While most people enjoy social media as a way to connect and keep in touch, hackers see it as a fantastic opportunity to gather the information needed for a hack.

- Now, make a list of the target's friends, download all of his posted information and images and make a duplicate "clone" profile. At this point, you can now begin to contact his friends and when they accept your friend request, you can begin to trade messages with them. This is the perfect way to get real inside information on the target's life. For instance, in John Doe's case, you send his friend a friend request, the friend begins talking with you thinking you're John and asks something like, so how's your fiancée Jane? Now, you know John Doe is engaged and you even know his fiancée's name!

- Remember, Facebook is simply crawling with false profiles, making it hard to spot the real from the faux. In order to ensure that you're really on your target's page, try this: Because Facebook uses the username located in the URL of your profile when you do a Facebook search bar search, it does so in this way: http://www.facebook.com/john.doe73 ;

- In this case "john.doe73" is John Doe's username. Now, this technique enables you to guess John Doe's email identification in the following way: Head to the Facebook login page and select "Forgot Password". You'll see "Find Your Account" with an option to enter your email, phone, username or full name into the bar.

- Choose username as the option, fill in john.doe and hit search.

- You will be directed to a page that says "Reset Your Password" and below, asks you how you would like to reset your password.

- An option to "email me a link to my password" shows up. Select this and it will show the user's email with the middle obfuscated with stars, like this: j******e@gmail.com. Congratulations!

You now have your target's name and you know that he uses Gmail.

- Now, examine the email. Although the entire middle is hidden you can see that it starts with j and ends with e, with 6 characters in between. You can easily guess that the first part of the address includes the name "john doe" but there are only 7 characters so there must be something in the middle of the name. Remember that the target's username was john.doe? There was a dot in between the first and last name and that would fit perfectly here too so try that. You get john.doe@gmail.com.You can easily check for the existence of this email address by heading to a free email address verifying site online.

- If it exists, the verifying site will let you know that it is a real address, making you surer that you've got your target's email address.

- It's time to get more information by turning to LinkedIn. You can scour your target's profile for details on his profession, location, education and past employment. Facebook and LinkedIn should be able to provide you with ample information, but if you need to go a step further, try a tool like the harvester to collect additional details about John Doe.

- At this point, you have:

  Target's First and Last name: John Doe (Theoretically)

  Address: Los Angeles, California (Theoretically)

  Occupation: Architect (Theoretically)

  Place of Employment: J Designs (Theoretically)

  Email ID: john.doe@gmail.com (Theoretically)

  Facebook Username: john.doe (Theoretically)

- It's now the right time to make contact with Mr. John Doe at this point. Equipped with his location and profession, you would look for a large architecture firm in LA. Then you would create an amazing job opportunity at a major company and send him this offer. Most likely, he'd jump at the chance.

- During your search for a large architectural firm based in Los Angeles, you likely came up with plenty of options. You would choose one firm and search that firm's website for the email ID of their hiring department. For this purpose, numerous fake emailing services exist, allowing you to send an illegitimate message impersonating the firm you chose.

- If your firm's name was "LA firm", your "firm's" email ID would be hiring@LA firm.com .

- You'd draft an email, inviting him to apply for a well-paid position at this "firm" and making sure that the "position's" requirements match your target's skills, education and employment history.

- As a final social engineering touch, you would mention that the opening is urgent and you'd need to hear from him promptly to consider his application. Why would you do this? Humans believe that a good opportunity is a limited time opportunity. When faced with a deadline to try and get something good, we often throw caution to the wind and forget to ask questions. Hackers know this and use it against us in every social engineering hack.

- What happens next is astonishing. The target, Mr. John Doe is delighted by the opportunity and quickly sends his resume to the fictitious hiring department. As you know, a resume is packed with all kinds of personal and even confidential information, providing hackers with a treasure trove to work with.

- If you performed this process, you would have just ended up successfully retrieving a whole slew of useful private information, equipping yourself to either social engineer your target further in a financial scam or to steal his identity.

This is all theoretical and while it's obvious that YOU would never do that, most black hat hackers have no moral scruples about pulling exactly this kind of a scam on an unsuspecting victim who is happy to have received such a "good" job offer.

Hopefully, this has illustrated for you just how dangerous AND easy social engineering hacking truly is.

Now, let's say that you've gotten some pretty useful information from Mr. John Doe but you haven't gotten everything you need. What's next?

More email communication with you playing the role of the hiring department chief at the "firm" you're pretending to be from will net you exactly what you're looking for. Malicious hackers know that most of us have become aware about hacking to a certain extent and they've come up with some truly cunning methods to social engineer their way into our systems and lives. One of these methods is to "continue communication" long enough to establish a certain level of trust between them and the target, then BAM! Before the target knows what's happened, the hacker has gone off with his or her information. By the time the target realizes that they've been hacked, it's usually too late to recover from the damage done to his or her finances, safety and reputation.

When it comes to Mr. John Doe, he may have given you his phone number, specific address and plenty of other valuable information but chances are, he won't have his Social Security number on the resume he sent to your "firm". In order to get this, you may have to create an attachment file "company profile" that disguises a malicious backdoor executable.

This would then be emailed to the target, ostensibly to let him know more about "the LA Firm". He would most likely click it open immediately, eager to learn more about the company that wants to hire him.

As soon as he opens the attachment, he'd be unknowingly giving you full access to his device, making it easy for you to capture credit card and bank account information, his Social Security number-basically all of his personal data.

Sometimes, hackers try a different approach. Equipped with the knowledge of the target "John Doe's" social and work contacts culled from a search of Facebook and LinkedIn, the hacker may send an executable file with a trustworthy or helpful-sounding name to the target. Because the hacker used a name from among the target's list of friends in the email and because the file was given a "safe" name, the target is likely to trust it and run it.

 The executable file will actually be part of a backdoor executable hack and once the target runs it, it will give the hacker an entry point to the target's device.

This hack melds careful pretexting social engineering techniques with classic hacking and is a clear example of just how dangerous it is to open an email or run anything from an "unknown" source, no matter how trustworthy it may seem.

Let's take a look at this type of hack. This is a little more complex than the previous hack we just detailed but don't worry, we'll go through it step-by-step!

Social Engineering Hack #2: How to Create a Backdoor Executable

This hack involves the creation of a payload executable and listener in Social engineering Toolkit (also known as SET). We'll get the Social Engineering Toolkit with Metasploit.

Next, we'll make the executable appear to be a clean Kaspersky executable by using Resource Hacker. Lastly, we'll put the entire package together using a WinRAR download.

The Goal of This Hack:

This hack's ultimate goal is to send the hacking target ("Mr. John Doe") a safe-looking but secretly malicious executable file that he will then unwittingly run on his device. A hacker does this by first making a listener and payload then turning it into an executable with a proper, seemingly trustworthy icon and then putting the whole thing together with WinRAR. Using WinRAR, a data compression tool, will allow the package to easily get past anti-viruses.

The final step is sending and allowing "John Doe" to run it. The hacker then is phoned once everything goes active.

Items You'll Need For This Hack:

- Social Engineering Toolkit That Comes With Metasploit

- WinRAR

- The Latest Debian-Derived Security Linux Distribution

- Resource Hacker

Step 1: First, you type "msfconsole" into a terminal window. The required Metasploit modules will now load. (**Hacker Tip:** For the newest versions of exploits and modules, don't forget to run msfupdate.)

After the loading is completed, you type in "**cd \pentest\exploits\set**" and hit enter. Now, the Social Engineering Toolkit will load.

Step 2: From the menu, choose **1** for Social-Engineering Attacks and hit enter. Another menu showing options will then appear. Choose 4-Create a Payload and Listener from this menu and hit enter.

Step 3: In order to put together the payload and listener, you'll now enter some parameters.

You'll be asked to enter the IP address for the payload. For example, if the IP address is "112.233.44.55" (This is just a theoretical made-up one for example purposes) you'd enter this and hit enter. This will then bring up a menu of various exploit options. In this tutorial, you'll be using the TCP/IP Reverse Shell exploit.

Step 4: Choose 1 "Windows Shell Reverse_TCP" and hit enter. This will spawn a command shell before sending back to attacker. A new menu will then show up inquiring about the encoding type to use to get past an anti-virus. Choose number 16- "BEST (Backdoored

Executable). Hit enter. Now, you'll be asked to choose the port for the listener.

Whichever port is fine but here go ahead and choose 1337, input it and hit enter. This allows the listener to be created and in the meantime, type "yes" to answer the question: "Start the listener now?"

Step 5: Upon completion, the executable file will be stored in**"/pentest/exploits/set/src/program_jun k".** The payload has now been created. The next step is to pull from a normal Microsoft executable file in order to have an icon image for the exploit.

Step 6: This stage is important and involves taking an icon image from Kaspersky Scanner file for your exploit.

Items You'll Need for This Stage:

- A program that you want to pull the icon from-in this case, let's use Kaspersky Security Scanner

- Resource Hacker

Step 7: In Resource Hacker, head to File, then Open. Next, find the file you need the icon from.

In this case, go ahead and employ the Kaspersky Security Scanner icon. Open the .exe file of the Kaspersky Security Scanner and a list of icons with plus symbols beside each will appear. Find the icon you want to pull and click the plus that is next to it. Then, click the plus beside 1. This will reveal the icons in this executable.

Step 8: Now that you've got the icon you want, right click on its file and choose Save [Icon] Resources. You'll bind this icon with the Metasploit backdoor command shell that you made earlier in stage 1 of this hack through WinRAR.

Stage 3: Disguising With WinRAR

This final stage involves putting the backdoor executable and icon together and disguising it with a "safe" icon using WinRAR.

Items You'll Need for This Stage:

• A Copy of WinRAR

Step 9: First, place together in a folder the backdoor executable you made and the icon you pulled in previous stages. Give it any name you prefer. Highlight the 2 files and right click. Next, choose the "Add to Archive" option. The Archive Name and Parameters window will appear at this point.

Step 10: In The Archive Name and Parameters window, put in the name you'd like the executable file to be names. For the purposes of this tutorial, let's call it SecurityScanner.exe. Next, check "Create SFX Archive" and then check "Create Solid Archive".

Step 11: From the drop down menu found below "Compression Method", choose "Best". Finally, head to the top of the screen and click on "Advanced Tab".

Step 12: Here, click "SFX Options". Click "Setup" in the new window that appears. Put in your executable's name "SecurityScanner.exe" (or whatever you choose) under "Setup". It should be under the option "Run after Extraction".

Step 13: Click "Modes" and under it check "Unpack to temporary Folder". Beside "Hide all" choose the radio button in order to allow the backdoor to run without alerting your target.

Step14: In order to bind the backdoor and the pulled icon together, click "Text and

Icon". Now, choose "Browse" under "Load SFX Icon from the File". Go to the Kaspersky Scanner icon file, head to the bottom and click "OK". This allows WinRAR to perform its function.

Congratulations! You'll find your new executable file, complete with pulled icon in the directory. You've just learned how to create backdoor, make it look like something else and then put it all together.

Now, this was a theoretical tutorial but if a malicious hacker was using this process, he or she would utilize the kinds of social engineering we discussed in this chapter. The last step would be to find the perfect way "in" by crafting a believable and compelling reason for the target to run the executable file.

Everyone is vulnerable to social engineering in one way or another. With the rise of people confessing almost every single detail of their lives on social media sites like Twitter and Facebook as well as professional network sites such as LinkedIn, this vulnerability is only increasing. Now that you've taken a look at the most common of the many ways a hacker can social engineer their way into your world, using both human-driven and computer-driven techniques, it's clear that you need to work towards putting up a very strong defense system in the face of this onslaught.

As I promised, this book is not only about gaining access to the murky secrets of the hackers of the dark web. It's also about learning how to protect yourself from these secrets and keeping yourself and your loved ones safe from the ever –present threat of a hacking campaign. So without further ado, take a look at this list of the most effective things you need to start doing RIGH NOW, to avoid being socially engineered.

The Most Effective Ways to Avoid Being the Victim of a Social Engineering Hack:

1. Be Aware: Just knowing about all of the different scams and tricks that hackers use to socially engineer their way past security protocols can contribute to your safety, so keep yourself updated about the latest developments in social engineering hacks, for greater security. Staying in a state of alertness will help you to remember that "friendly" strangers who try to join your social network or out of the blue job opportunities may not be as genuine as they first appear.

2. Stay Private: This era of "sharing" every single feeling, event and detail on Social media is a hacker's dream and a hacking target's nightmare. While I'm certainly not saying that you can't enjoy connecting with people online, it's vital to remember that hackers are always present in the background, watching and noticing your posts, your conversations and images. They are looking for everything from the city you live in to what your hobbies are, and they end up using these facts against you in some truly terrifying ways. So don't let yourself become the next owned target. Keep private information such as your exact location within your circle of friends by not making your page viewable to just anyone. Selecting the privacy setting on Facebook will help keep you and your loved ones much safer. In the same vein, don't hand out ANY information about yourself over the phone to an unknown person, no matter who they claim to be. Hackers will often call you posing as help desk operators and ask you for sensitive details. Even if you have reason to believe that the call is genuine, always verify before sharing any details, whether you think the information is confidential or not. Keep in mind that help desk employees

and those calling from your credit card provider or bank will never ask you to provide any confidential or sensitive personal information during a phone call.

3. Use Your Shredder: Hackers will often follow up online stalking campaigns with dumpster diving, meaning that if you dispose of any of your private papers without ever properly tearing them up, they can quickly get their hands on all the details they need to steal your money or your identity. There are plenty of news headlines about people being hacked because of the information found on a forgotten receipt. So switch on that shredder and get rid of anything that bears even a minimum of information about you.

4. Create Secure Passwords, Have a Different Login for Every Service and Use Two-Factor Authentication: Avoid the biggest internet security mistake of all, having one password for more than one account. Create unique, difficult to crack passwords that are mix of numbers, letters and symbols. Using two-factor authentication discourages criminal beak-ins to your accounts, despite any passwords or usernames being stolen.

5. **Be Smart About How You Use Credit Cards:** Credit is still king and credit cards are definitely far safer than PayPal or debit cards as an online payment method. For example, a hacker can easily hack your debit card account number and take all of the money. However, failing to use your cards wisely could also leave you in a world of trouble. Make sure that you keep your money safe by never leaving your credit card number stored on a site. You can always use the excellent option throw-away cards when shopping online.

6. **Don't Let Your Private Information Go Public:** Hackers love to use public information databases whenever they are laying the groundwork for a social engineering hack. This is because these databases do all of the hard work for them, amassing huge amounts of potentially sensitive information about a wide range of people and displaying it online for anyone who wants to see it. So what can you do if you're name and information appears on one of these databases like People Finders? Well, there are plenty of other resources online that effectively help you to figure out where you are mentioned and also provide the ability to remove your personal information

such as name, address, marital status and others, from these databases.

7. **Do Regular Periodic Checks of Your Personal Data and Accounts:** Keeping a sharp eye on your accounts and your personal information is a great way of finding out about a hack even while it is in progress. Google Alerts can help with this. Many people just ignore their credit score assuming that it is the same until they actually need to use it for a major purchase. That's when people often find out for the first time that they have been hacked. Don't let this happen to you. Always look carefully at credit card and back account statements as well as examining your credit score regularly for any changes.

8. **Always Backup Your Information:** In case a social engineering hack actually hits you, you'll want to make sure that despite hackers controlling your device, your data, at least, won't be completely lost.

Remember that while this interconnected age means that 100 % complete safety is not really possible, you are not powerless in the face of social engineering techniques. Using the methods I outlined above will help you stay one step ahead of any of the many malicious social engineering scams that hackers may attempt to hit you with.

Join me in the next chapter, where we'll be examining one of the most disturbing threats to emerge from the dark web in recent years and what you can do to make sure it doesn't do any damage to you!

Chapter 8:
The BlackShades RAT - How to Protect Yourself From the Enemy Within the Gates!

Imagine coming home, opening up and turning on your computer and finding that,instead of the familiar startup display, you have a large threatening ransom message that says something along these lines:

"WARNING! Make sure that you read this message for your own good. We have taken over your computer and encrypted all of your data and information. We are the only ones who can decrypt your data and send it back to you again safely. If you ever want to get this data back safe and sound, you must follow our instructions. If you do not, all of our information and data will immediately be destroyed!"

These instructions would then include a bank account and advise you to pay a certain amount of money into the stated account, in the hopes that you may retrieve your lost information, photos, videos, addresses and other sensitive data. Even if you do pay however, there is no guarantee that you will get your information back or that the hackers who stole it in the first place won't hold on to it as a bargaining chip to blackmail you into to forking over even more money.

This ransom note is a common tool used by hackers today and is exactly what thousands of people have found on their screens in recent years, as a dangerous new hacking threat emerges.

A malevolent new tool in the dark world of hacking has made it possible for strangers millions of miles away or right next door to watch your every move, record your private moments and conversations, encrypt your data and basically hold you hostage. This tool isn't some strange far-fetched idea from a sci-fi movie. Instead, it is a very real threat, a malicious software program called BlackShades that is compromising the security of millions of computers globally.

So how does it work? This software program features a remote access trojan (aptly known as RAT, for short) which is a kind of malware that allows virtual criminals to completely breakdown your computer's security systems, conquer its programs and systems and watch you 24 hours a day. When a hacker installs BlackShades on your computer, it's the equivalent of getting wiretapped and kidnapped at the same time. This program is made up of two parts- A controller and a server. The hacker installs the server or program onto your device then takes complete control of your device's system via the controller. And just like with a real-life home invasion, these hackers and their dangerous program can't get in unless YOU let them in.

That's right. Almost 100% of the time, BlackShades is actually installed onto your device by your very own unwitting hands! Here's how it works: Just like with the ancient story of the Greeks sending an attack disguised as a gift to their opponents, the Trojan horse component of BlackShades and other malware programs are often presented to victims disguised as either harmless items or beneficial gifts. The most popular ways that hackers use to spread BlackShades (and other malware) include:

- **Phishing email scams which install the malware into your computer and swipe all of your secret information**

- **Social media and email password information.**

- **Fake torrent downloads on P2P sites**

- **Drive-bys**

- **Fake downloads**

- **Java exploits**

- **Malicious chat room links**

- **Malicious social media links shared on Facebook, Twitter and other platforms**

- **Hacked social media accounts**

Hackers use very sophisticated social engineering tactics to trick you into believing that you are clicking on and visiting a secure site or installing something beneficial, safe or useful. Instead, you are actually installing a nasty malware program and you're losing the ability to control your own device. Once you've been fooled into doing the dirty work for them by installing the software onto your own machine, the hacker can then begin to carry out his/her original plan: To control, watch and exploit you through your system. Here are just some of the terrifying ways in which a hacker can utilize Blackshades against you:

- To control your social media posts (especially on Facebook)

- To install a key-logging device which swipes and passes on all of your vital private passwords, credentials, account numbers and other secret information to the hacker controlling your device

- To store, host and distribute illegal files from your device, without your knowledge. Hackers often do this and avoid any fines or unwanted legal attention by storing THEIR illegal files on YOUR system, leaving you holding the bag if the authorities come knocking!

- To launch a ransomware attack against you by sending you the kind of message I discussed above and forcing you into paying major money by threatening to distribute your private information or destroy your valuable money if the specified ransom is not paid

- To draft your computer into a coordinated Distributed Denial of Service Attack (Also known as DOS) in which the hacker employs many kidnapped infected devices against a targeted server.

- To monitor and secretly record all of your activities through surveillance and remote controlled screenshots

- To take over your device's webcam

- To take over your MSN messenger feature

- To employ arbitrary code on your device (Enabling the hackers to execute any command they wish on your device, at any time!)

- To download and run files on your device

What do these cybercriminals gain from this, you may wonder? Well, the two main benefits to them are surveillance and profit. Perhaps you may hold the mistaken belief theat such a sophisticated and risky program is ulta-expensive and so high-tech that only a priviledged few can get their hands on it. I'm here to tell you that this belief is nothing more than wishful thinking, The fact is, the Blackshades RAT is accessible to anyone in the world, from a highschooler in your town to super-hacker in a far-away country, all for the incredibly low price of just 40 dollars!Even worse, the program is so easy to use that now anyone, anywhere with even a minimum of computer-knowledge can turn into an overnight top cybercriminal, ready and equipped to steal your data, capture your image and destroy your privacy.

In many cases, Blackshades is disguised as a "free Adobe Flash Player" or other free, useful "software". The minute you click on and install this "free" program, you are essentially playing right into the hands of the hacker, opening yourself up to be the latest victim of BlackShades file and system kidnapping. You'll quickly find yourself locked out of your own device and will have to pay a hefty fee to the hacker in order to get back in.

These and other mistakes are the reason why BlackShades is creating thousands of overnight hacking success stories. Anybody, anywhere can simply purchase the program for $40 or even get it from a hacking contact for free and in a matter of minutes, they can start sending out malicious links and taking over the devices of unsuspecting victims. This is a very lucrative business and hackers ae getting rich in a matter of weeks, making it very unlikely that the BlackShades attacks will stop anytime soon. Already thousands have been blackmailed and many more are being watched, recorded and listened to without knowing that their devices have been compromised. Unfortunately, just because you haven't received a ransom note yet doesn't mean that your device is in the clear. Often times, hackers will wait and watch you for many months, looking for important private information or data before openly attacking you. That's why it's so vital that you find out your devices status.

Have You Been Invaded By A BlackShades RAT?

While BlackShades can be a very sneaky and hard to detect malware program, these are the top signs that you may have a BlackShades problem on your hands:

- Does your webcam light suddenly switch on when you aren't using the camera?

- Is your system extremely sluggish to start up or while running?

- Has it become impossible for you to access your computer files because of data encryption?

- Does your mouse cursor move strangely, without you moving it?

- Does your display suddenly become dark while you are using it?

- Do text chat windows suddenly and erratically pop up on your device's screen?

- Has someone changed your account passwords without your knowledge or compromised your usernames or passwords?

- Have you received a ransom note such as the one mentioned above, instructing you to pay money in order to be able to access your files?

If the answer to one or more of these questions is yes, then there is a high probability that you're dealing with a device infected by BlackShades. So all you need to do is find out and get rid of it, right? This may sound easy but in fact, BlackShades is designed to conceal its presence in your device so expertly that it's often extremely difficult to find it. But as I promised you, we don't just deal with doom and gloom in this book, we actually provide real answers and solutions. That's why I've compiled a list of files that indicate a definite BlackShades infection in your device for you to use. If you do a hard drive search for ***.bss** files and find:

- dos_sock.bss

- nir_cmd.bss

- pws_cdk.bss

- pws_chro.bss

- pws_ff.bss

- pws_mail.bss

- pws_mess.bss

If you find any of these files in the course of your search, then you can be 100% sure that your device has been infected by BlackShades and that you must eliminate this infection right away! Because BlackShades is particularly tricky, I recommend using a well-known anti-malware tool to scan and remove it. Always remember to disconnect your internet connection after the initial installation of your selected anti-malware tool. This will help to ensure that the hacker behind your BlackShades infection doesn't have the opportunity to mess with your elimination actions. If your information has been "kidnapped" by the BlackShades hackers and has been lost or deleted, you should bring your device to a good computer forensics technician, in order to try to retrieve it.

Next, you will want to make sure that you change all of your passwords and usernames because often, the first thing a hacker does after using BlackShades to enter your system is to collect this information and breach your accounts. After you make these changes, also keep a very sharp eye on your credit cards and back accounts to make sure that the hackers are not siphoning off funds, using the account information that they gathered during your infection.

The best way to guarantee that your device remains BlackShades-free is to be smart and super-critical about the emails you receive. If you see a blank email with just a link, DON"T click the link. Chances are you'll be opening the door to a nasty infection. Instead, delete the email right away and report it your email server. The same goes for attachments from unknown sources. Regardless of how interesting the title or heading, resist your curiosity and hit delete. Because BlackShades specializes in disabling your anti-virus and anti-malware software, make sure that you're keeping this software updated, to put up a robust defense. Always keep your OS(operating system) updated as well as updating all of the programs running on your system and never, EVER install unknown or unfamiliar software on your device.

And lastly but not least, remember that a large number of hackers using BlackShades are doing so in order to watch and record you in your private, unguarded moments. Many people have been blackmailed by these BlackShades Hackers who threaten to share or post these personal images if they don't receive a big pay-out.

Make this ploy impossible for them by simply switching off your computer when not in use and don't forget to cover your webcam with a strip of dark tape. Sometimes the easiest anti-hacking tips really are the most useful!

Chapter 9:
Learn How Easy it Really Is to Become a Millionaire Hacker

While many aspects of the hacking world are kept tightly under wraps by the citizens of the dark web, there is one secret that they just can't keep hidden from the rest of us: There is serious money in hacking-lots of it.

In a world where the average college graduate can barely scrape enough to manage a living wage, there are is now a growing number of motivated, self-taught hackers who have no degrees and no certifications but are still able to make as much as $90,000 a month!

That's right, even mid-level hackers can easily pull in close to a hundred grand every 30 days, with no more effort than it would take to hold down a normal job! By this point, I'm sure you're wondering how? Well, all it really requires is a good basic level of hacking knowledge, a complete disregard for rules and regulations and a keen sense of human nature's weak spots. Hackers need the 1st two attributes in order to achieve anything in the hacking world because quite frankly, without a certain level of knowledge about computer systems and how to utilize their weaknesses for gain, a hacker will just end up as a script kiddie and if they let hang-ups about the rules of the internet get in the way, they'll never be able to make the massive amounts of money on offer on the illicit computer underground.

The 3rd attribute, knowledge of human nature and its habits, weaknesses and foibles, is an essential trait because without it, a hacker can never pull off the daring and often complex social engineering scams that they regularly do. Getting people to trust your hack is the biggest hack of all.

With these 3 attributes, a black hat hacker can literally become a self-made millionaire in a very short period of time. Now, I understand that this may be hard to believe. After all, Ivy Leaguers aren't pulling in those types of figures a year, let alone a month. But the truth is, if you look at the math, you will quickly see that I've actually **_understated_** how much the average skilled hacker can make in a month. Let's take a look at the real numbers:

The Breakdown:

- On average, redirects hit at least 25,000 users a day.

- Exploit kits used by hackers are successful about 10% of the time.

- When victims are hit with ransomware, an estimated 0.5% of them will end up paying to get their device and their personal data back.

- On average, hackers tend to ask their victims for at least $500 as a ransom payment. However, just to prove to you that these facts are solid and not exaggerated in any way, let's make it $300.

Now, in order to calculate how much the average hacker will make from the simple ransomware hack that is so popular right now, simply multiply 25,000(victims of redirects) by 10%(the average success rate) then multiply the result by 0.5%(the usual percent of people who pay the ransom) and finally multiply this by $300(approximate ransom price).You'll get $3750 a day. If you multiply this by 30 days, you'll see that the average ransomware-using hacker can make a whopping $112,500 a month.

Of course, with hacking, as with any other enterprise, there are some costs doing to doing business. These include paying approximately

$3500 a month for the payload to be used in the hacks, then another $700 per month for payload obfuscation. An exploit kit will set hackers back about $500 per month and for traffic, they can expect to pay up to $1800 per month. Add all of this up to get the total monthly cost of carrying out the business of ransomware hacks and you'll see that it's only $6500. Even with this deduction, the hacker ends up with a very nice tidy sum of $106,000 on a monthly basis.

Once you see these numbers, it becomes a lot easier to understand why so many people, from beginners to top professionals, are putting so much time and energy into learning as much about hacking as possible!

The RIG Exploit Kit Hack

The RIG Exploit Kit is one of the most beloved methods for hackers to make large amounts of money in a short space of time. This exploit kit is utilized to place threats onto the devices of unsuspecting users.

Most recently, hackers have been using the RIG Exploit Kit to install different types of Trojans, including Cryptolockers. This exploit kit allows hackers to bypass the security measures that prevented Cryptolocker from taking hold on devices and works by encrypting files on users' devices and then pulling the familiar ransomware hack. Using this popular hacking method, malicious hackers rake in massive amounts of money through money transfers sent by their desperate victims. Because the RIG Exploit Kit allows hackers to encrypt your files and makes decryption almost impossible without the key they utilized in the encryption process, the hackers can easily charge ransom payments as high as $600 per victim. Once even an amateur hacker gets his/her hands on this exploit kit, they can basically start raking in the profits.

If you happened to be a hacker who became a RIG manager with as few as 500 customers who pay you only $120 in rent every week, you end up making a cool $60,000 a week. While to most people, that's a pretty decent annual salary, to a mid-level hacker with enough skill to circumvent security and social engineer victims, that's just small change! Some elite black hat hackers even make over $100,000 a month by employing this system.

At this point, the RIG Exploit Kit has infected nearly 1.3 million PCS (about 30,000 PCs a day), making it extremely easy for malicious hackers to turn a great profit using it.

The Network: The Credentials Black Hat Hackers Must Have to Play at the Big Money Table:

The hacking world is very similar to a large Las Vegas casino. There are many levels of skill, expertise, investment and reward, just as there are different levels of games in a casino, ranging from the lowly coin slots machines, to the regular tables all the way up to the VIP high stakes tables in the back, for the big spenders. In the same way, the dark web hosts groups that are only available to select members of the hacking world, depending on your reputation, status, financial abilities and hacking proficiency. In order to get into the very exclusive "club" of hackers who make millions of dollars a year, you have to be known and accepted by the other members of that group. For example, the RIG Exploit Kit hack requires specific knowledge and access to exploit kits or tools that are secretly traded on a shady underground black market online for cyber-criminals.

However, no one is just going to let you saunter into one of these black markets and simply buy whatever exploit kit you want. Instead, you have to be recommended by an existing hacker within the circle or have a reputation for malicious hacking that lets the other members know you're not a script kiddie or someone looking to expose the black market's secrets. So what are these circles like? Well, the closest example for them is that they are like Craigslist or other trading forums but they are much more strictly guarded and are open to only the best or most well-known hackers. Once you've been able to gain entry to one of these circles you can easily buy illicit pre-made exploits to use in hacking feats, helping you to make a huge amount of money, even if you aren't the best or most advanced hacker on the field. While hacking is often a private endeavor, with the rise of these groups, a certain brotherhood of malicious hacking has developed and now, the hacking world has become much more like a normal industry, with each hacker buying, selling and providing required services to another. Security in these circles is tight and hackers do everything possible to thwart outsiders and safeguard these groups, because they make so much money out of the information and equipment they buy and sell in them.

DDoS: The Hacker's Get-Rich Quick Scheme:

DDoS, or distributed denial of service campaigns, are one of the main ways that malicious hackers target companies and make millions in the process. Hackers can coordinate huge DDoS campaigns against one organization's servers flooding those servers with hundreds of billions of bits of data every single second. And these campaigns are not being run for the fun of it. Instead, there are literally thousands of elite malicious hackers around the world who are making millions of dollars from DDoS campaigns as you read this. But how are these hackers making these huge paydays? They have created a system in which they first take numerous devices captive through a Trojan infection. Then they use these devices in order to create a chain or network of unwilling but trapped computers referred to as botnets. The botnets are then used to overwhelm specifically targeted servers with DDoS, or distributed denial of service campaigns, ultimately bringing down their intended victims. These centrally manipulated chains of PCs carry out DDoS activities, sending gargantuan amounts of traffic volume to servers and websites. These websites and servers are then put out of commission for a certain amount of time.

Top hackers own powerful botnet networks and loan them out to those who want to bring certain servers to their knees and are more than happy to pay well for them. Anyone, whether it's someone out for financial gain, revenge or simply wanting to harm a competing business, can rent a botnet for as little as half an hour at a time and use them to blackmail a company or organization. If the organization pays up, the botnets will stop sending overwhelming traffic to their servers or websites and their normal operations will resume. Notorious hackers have explained that they can make someone's monthly salary in just a few hours of running botnet DDoS campaigns and that they can do this all while relaxing on a couch. The kingpins of these operations are usually elite level hackers.

However, if you can get your hands on the automated tools to create your own botnet chain, you too can launch this distributed denial of service campaigns and make a hefty salary of your own, even WITHOUT any expert technical know-how. Recently, a certain section of the public has become more aware of malicious DDoS campaigns and software has been created to ward them off but those who persist in sending these hack attacks still stand to gain. Most companies remain vulnerable to DDoS launches because they don't usually purchase the protection they need and end up having to fork out thousands of dollars in one day to try to get their servers back up and running.

The Blackmail Hack:

Particularly sophisticated hackers are also involved in the blackmailing of major corporations for large paydays. While the headlines are full of hackers who make their money by plundering the credit card details of unsuspecting customers from huge chain stores, online shopping sites, banks and other businesses, many of the very best hackers are actually silently launching another kind of hack- the company blackmail ploy., also known as organizational cyber extortion. This kind of hacking technique makes a great deal of sense because most companies are very wary of negative publicity and will do almost anything a hacker asks of them in order to make bad press go away. According to the most conservative estimates, at least $5 million a year are paid out by victims of cyber extortion to hackers. And this threat is only growing. Because of relatively simple malicious programs available online for anyone to access, your business or personal life could be ransacked by a beginner hacker.

Recently, a group of dark web hackers has been breaking down the strong security protocols of banks and managing to hack into all of their customers' confidential information. These groups then inform the banks that unless they are paid almost $200,000 by a set day and time, they will release this sensitive information. Because this would irreparably destroy a bank's credibility with its customers, the targeted banks are almost always willing to quietly pay the money and the hackers also keep up their end of the bargain, in order to ensure that the next target is willing to pay, as well. These blackmail campaigns are growing more and more brazen, with hackers hitting out at major conglomerates and mom and pop establishments. These hackers often knock out a company's website before putting it back online about 20 minutes later. They then send their victims an email posing as an ethical "white hat "hacker who has specialist knowledge in cyber security and "discovered" a vulnerability in the company's security or a bug in their software. Instead of an out-and-out ransom demand, these hackers will send a more subtle message: "I can fix your problem, for the right price." This is just a smooth way of telling the organization that they have no choice but to pay the hacker, if they want to regain and maintain their data, functionality and security. There are now special types of ransomware software designed by elite black hat hackers that are designed to specifically target corporate computers. Even keeping in mind that only about 0.5% of those victimized actually end up paying the hackers, when one hacker is target many thousands of devices through a botnet chain, there is still quite a large fortune to be made. One hacker even kept a doctor locked out of the medical records of his patients, while offering to "patch" the vulnerability for about $50,000!

Chapter 10:
Computer Hacking and Identity Theft - How Expert Hackers Could Literally Steal Your Life in a Couple of Clicks!

Imagine this: You wake up one morning, check your phone and realize that your inbox is stuffed full with nervous voicemails and texts from your friends and family-they're wondering if you're okay and want to know where to send the money you asked them for in your group email. Obviously, you have no idea what they're talking about so you check your email, Facebook account and other social media and guess what-You can't get in! Your passwords have all been changed, effectively locking you out of your own accounts! At this point, you're panicking but you pull yourself together and go to work. Once there, you find that things are much worse than you initially guessed.

Your colleagues are all looking at you strangely and your boss calls you into his office and asks you to explain the insulting emails you've been sending to everyone at work! At this point, things may seem pretty bad but your nightmare is only just beginning-you have become one of the many people around the world who have had their identities stolen by malicious hackers.

Hackers can do so much more than contact and extort your friends and family while pretending to be you, send messages to your colleagues and even your boss and lock you out of your online accounts. They can actually get their hands on your bank account and credit card information and either slowly drain your funds or else quickly drain all of your money in one swift go.

In the past, identity thieves used to be fairly unsophisticated-mostly pickpockets and credit card thieves. These days, the growing rise of identity theft is being fueled by criminal hacking rings. They are anything but unsophisticated. In fact, they are highly skilled, disciplined and well-organized and they are out to get your information, your money and ultimately your life.

Because identity theft has become as easy as taking candy from a baby, a hacker need not be a professional identity thief in order to make the huge money that comes from this hack. In fact, thousands of people have been hacked by and lost their identities to complete amateurs. This ease of operation makes identity theft hacking very lucrative, accessible and very, very dangerous. Consider these facts:

- Hacking is claiming a greater share of all data breaches reported

- Over 43 million Americans have been directly affected by hacking and identity theft in the last year alone.

- Both private individuals and enormous companies have been attacked by computer hackers who have stolen information and used it to impersonate, extort or rob many.

- With the increasing connectivity of modern life, experts believe that hacking will inevitably be the most common crime of the future.

In the face of such facts, the biggest single mistake you could possibly make is to believe that it could never happen to you. The fact is, with its widespread nature, this type of hacking can and does happen often and to a large cross section of the population. If you want to avoid the terrible experience of having your personal information rifled through, stolen and used against you, you must be proactive. Carrying on with business as usual will eventually lead to falling prey to a vicious case of identity theft hacking.

Computer identity theft takes place in several ways:

Large scale criminal hacker rings either use their own hackers, pay promising young amateur hackers to do the dirty work for them or they simply go the easy route and buy stolen information in bulk from hackers who are engaged in the identity trade.

The Most Common Hacking Methods For Identity Theft Include:

- Breaking into devices that have weak or non-existent firewalls

- Guessing and exploiting weak passwords, passwords used across several accounts or passwords stored within devices

- Installation of malicious code including keystroke loggers via a tainted link or attachment

- Exploiting weaknesses in browsers

- Disguising malicious code on websites

- Disguising malicious code in freely offered software or downloads

- Allowing outsiders to use your unprotected computer

- Wi-Fi networks exploitation

This list is by no means exhaustive and there are several new hacks being identified every day, but these are the biggest threats facing most users today.

When a Hacker Takes Over Your Phone:

Perhaps one of the scariest moments of being hacked is finding out that you no longer have access to or control over your phone. Hackers often work by cracking your password, bypassing your phone's security in order to register a different sim card on your account. Because most people never believe that they will ever be hacked, they often don't bother coming up with strong passwords for their phone accounts or changing those passwords regularly. When this happens, the hacker then keeps you out of your phone, while answering your calls, dialing your contact list, sending texts on your behalf and just generally causing mayhem and confusion in your life.

When a Hacker takes over Your Email Account:

Often, you can access your cell phone contacts through your email account-that is, if you can get into your account in the first place. Most hackers will use your phone number and other hacked information to break into your email and reset your password. You will receive an email on your backup account informing you that you have successfully changed your password on another account. As I'm sure you've noticed, the message also tells you that if you aren't the person who made this password change, you should follow the instructions provided, in order to change your password again. The real problem here-most email accounts will send you a verification code for password resets via your cell phone, and as you know, the hacker is the one in control of your phone now. You can't see the verification code and so you can't reset your password and reenter your email account!

So just how does a hacker enter your email account? Well, it's pretty simple actually. This hack is one of the most popular of all hacks and is very simple to pull off for even a total amateur **with no coding or hacking knowledge.**

Here is how it works:

First, the hacker sends a text to your phone, from an unknown number. This text asks you to verify your account by responding by sending the verification they send you. This is ostensibly to help check that your email account is secure but in reality, the verification code is actually a code that resets your password. The hacker then sends another message to the phone. This message has an unlock code. What happens next is a very click hack. You receive a text message claiming to be from your email provider, warning you that abnormal or unauthorized activity has been spotted on your account. They then tell you to send the verification code.

The moment you actually do as they ask, your email address slips out of your control and becomes the missing piece, allowing the hacker to log into your account completely unnoticed.

Because of the day and age we live in where companies are constantly sending us messages and many actions can be performed through a simple text, it's easy to be tricked into believing that the message is legitimate. This scam is used by hackers against popular email account providers like Yahoo, Gmail, Outlook and others. To avoid this hack, it's important to always keep yourself in a hacker's state of mind. What are hackers looking for? Information, more importantly, private information-and once you realize this, you start to see that any sudden messages or requests for even a small piece of that information must be viewed with extreme suspicion. In this case, keep in mind that any real password recovery service will never ask for a response from you when sending you a verification code.

What You Can Do to Protect Yourself From Becoming the Latest Phone Hack Victim:

1. Never, EVER respond to a verification request sent via the phone by texting back a code or anything else.

2. Remove your mobile phone number from all email signatures, even your business email signature. This will help to ensure that hackers don't view you as a sitting duck and use your number to initiate a hack.

3. Make sure that you aren't sliding by on the same old weak passwords for your email accounts. Always avoid using the same password across several accounts

unless you want to make yourself into a hacker's fantasy. Switch your passwords out for strong ones and never store them in your device.

4. Use the 2 step authentication process for all of your email accounts.

5. Go through each of your email accounts and look for any mail that contains sensitive information that hackers are typically seeking such as phone numbers, bank account and credit card information and ID numbers. Delete this information and if possible, change it to prevent hackers from using it against you.

Chapter 11:
How Hackers Can Steal Your Credit Card Information

If you have even checked your credit card statement and noticed unfamiliar charges that you know you didn't make, you likely already know just how frightening a credit card hack can be.

Hackers frequently hack into the systems of businesses, not only to target the businesses themselves, but also to scour for the thousands of credit card numbers of their clients. In the hacker world, retrieving credit card numbers is the equivalent of hitting the jackpot. The hacker can either directly siphon off money from the victim's account OR even more dangerously, sell the credit card information to other hacking groups halfway across the globe.

In this scenario, the original hacker gets paid a hefty sum for the credit card numbers, the global cyber-criminals who buy the numbers from the hacker can then use them to steal from individuals while remaining in anonymity in other countries –everyone wins!

Everyone, that is, except the victims of credit card hacks. If this sounds like something you never want to experience, you have to be hyper-aware of the new landscape of theft. Gone are the days when someone had to physically steal money from your pocket or run off with your purse. Today a hacker can empty out your bank accounts and leave you in complete shock and despair without ever even showing his or her face.

In recent years, over half of all US adults have been the target of a hack of some kind and out of those, many also had their credit card information stolen and illegally used. In the infamous Target Store hack of 2014 alone, hackers made over 53.7 million dollars from selling the information they stole from 2 million Target Customers' credit cards. It's a scary new world of financial crime and you've got to be properly equipped with information in order to avoid being one of the helpless millions affected.

Hackers pull off credit card number hacks in several ways, all of which are important to know about, in order to protect yourself or your company from the consequences:

These include:

Credit Card Hack # 1: The Phishing and Spoofing Scam:

The classic phishing and spoofing scam has long been a favorite of hackers because it takes very minimal effort on their part and offers quick rewards. In this scam, a hacker may email you with an official template that looks identical to the one used by your bank. The email will inform you that suspicious activity has been noticed in your account and that your bank believes that someone may be illegally accessing and using your funds. The email will direct you to log in to a site (with a helpful link provided!) in order to verify your identity by typing in your full bank account information. According to the email, this will help your bank shut the fraudulent user out of your account. Most people are so panicked by seeing an official email from their "bank" informing them that a stranger is stealing their money that they simply don't think twice about following the given instructions.

If, for some reason, you aren't panicky enough to instantly click the link, the hackers will even follow up with an official sounding phone call, repeating the same information to you and urging you to take action before the imaginary criminal steals even more of your money! 9 times out of 10, people who have reservations about believing the email will end up falling for the follow up phone call. Why? Simply put, it's just good social engineering.

Hackers know that people trust people. By adding the human touch and calling sounding like a trustworthy, concerned bank employee, they are betting that you will trust the "good person" on the other end of the line and follow their instructions. And their bet usually pays off! People who wouldn't dream of clicking a link and entering their account information online are more than willing to give that same information to a stranger posing as a bank employee over the phone!

That's why the phishing and spoofing combination is the scam that frequently nets hackers enormous pay day and empties more bank accounts in less time than any other financial scam out there.

Credit Card Hack #2: Direct Business Hacking:

Another method that hackers employ in order to steal credit card numbers is the direct business hack. Usually, hackers will break directly into a business' or many businesses' systems in search of clients' credit card numbers. If you've ever used an online commerce service to make purchases remotely, then you are familiar with their credit card systems. Often, to encourage and facilitate repeated purchases, these sites will allow you to log and store your credit card information with them in a "secure" manner.

They promise customers security by intensively encrypting all of the sensitive credit card information that customers give them. However, even though decryption of these credit card numbers is nearly impossible, as the old saying goes, "almost is only almost good enough." Hackers on the lookout for lucrative opportunities are constantly checking these sites out for weaknesses and when they find vulnerabilities, they never overlook the chance to exploit them. Instead, they immediately launch a hack that allows them to bypass the commerce site's or business' security measures and voila! They get their hands on thousands upon thousands of customers' credit card numbers and information.

It's the modern-day equivalent of the classic bank heist- the hackers slip past the site's "security guards" and enter the vault-usually without making any web chatter that would alert authorities. They make off with large amounts of cards in one go and neither the companies nor the customers are any wiser, until it's too late.

Credit Card Hack #3: Direct Individual Hacking:

When a hacker infects your device with malware, this gives him or her instant control over the information stored in it as well as the ability to read through your email accounts, log your key strokes, take screenshots of your computer activity and even watch and listen in on you at all times. This offers them a wide variety of ways to steal your credit card numbers among other sensitive personal information-whether it be logging as you use your card to make a purchase, reading messages in which your card number is mentioned or even recording your voice as you give credit card information over your phone.

Hackers often achieve this via "quiet" Trojan infections that sit tight in your system and send the hacker your data while you remain unsuspecting, because nothing has visibly charged on your device. By the time you realize that your credit card numbers have been hacked, it's usually at the point where the hacker has removed large sums of money from your accounts or even destroyed your good credit score, leaving you with bills you can't pay and damage you can't undo.

How to Avoid Being a Credit Card Hacker's Next Victim: These steps are designed to shield you from the risk:

1. Never give any credit card information during calls-no matter how official or concerned the caller sounds or how urgent they claim the situation is. If "your bank" is asking you to provide credit card information during a phone call, you can be sure that the call is being made by criminals. Hang up and call your bank (on the official number, not the number that just called you) and report the incident.

2. Never follow the instructions in a banking email that asks you to verify your identity by clicking on a link. This link is sure to take you to a fake duplicate site that will capture your sensitive information and pass it on to the hacker. Again, do not cooperate. Instead, call your bank directly for further information.

3. When it comes to shopping online, use single-use card numbers in order to thwart hackers who break into shopping sites' credit card database. If your credit

card doesn't support single-use card number technology, don't allow yourself to be lulled into a false sense of safety by the online shopping sites' promises of security. As of now, there is NO guarantee that these sites can provide you with a hacker-free shopping experience so don't store your credit card information with them. It may be less convenient but it is far safe to simply reenter the information yourself, every time you purchase online.

4. Avoid giving dangerous hackers control of your device, and by default, your credit card information, by resisting the urge to click on any unknown links in emails-even if they're from people you know. Malicious links in emails are one of the leading ways hackers use malware to usurp your private information.

While credit card theft is definitely increasing in scope and scale among both professional criminal hacking rings and talented amateur hackers, that doesn't mean that your card has to be the next prey. Taking the steps that I've outlined in this section can mean the difference between keeping your money and personal information safe or letting a malicious black hat hacker take control of your finances and your life.

Chapter 12:
The Social Security Hack from Hell: How Hackers Pull it Off and How to Prevent it From Happening to YOU!

Did you know that a hacker can steal your Social Security number in less than 60 minutes? When you think about just how important this information is and how many doors into your life it can open for a complete stranger, the knowledge that the average mid-level hacker can access it so easily is truly terrifying.

To help you see how this is possible, I want to first make one thing clear: Hundreds of high traffic website under the control of supposedly hack-proof institutions such as top banks and credit unions, universities and even US governmental sites actually contain major security vulnerabilities that could see your Social Security number being robbed by hackers.

Hard to believe, but unfortunately, all of these highly rusted institutions run websites that possess a number of weak points that hackers know about and regularly exploit to gain access to large loads of Social Security numbers at a time.

Below, I'll outline exactly how these hackers manage to pull this off:

In this type of hack, the hacker is essentially guessing. The hacker has a list of numbers and uses these to find yours through a process of elimination. A hacker basically asks the site on which your Social Security number is stored a series of question "messages". The best way to illustrate this process is like this:

The hacker asks the site:

Is "John Doe's" Social Security number 112-34-5678? If the reply is no, the hacker doesn't give up. He or she moves to the next estimated number on the list, asking: Is it 123-45-6789? If the answer is no again, the hacker simply moves onto the next possibility until a yes reply comes in.

Now, it's important to remember that the hacker is not asking these questions manually. Hackers use a script so basic that it could be written even by a low-level hacker, to send literally several thousand attempts to the site in just seconds. This means that even if the hacker has to try many thousands of attempts, he or she can still crack your Social Security number in less than 15 minutes!

Another factor that makes the process easier is that the hacker doesn't have to just pull these guesses out of thin air. Here's a secret that many people don't realize: ANYONE CAN PREDICT YOUR SOCIAL SECURITY NUMBER!

All Social Security numbers that were issued before June 2011 are to a certain extent, predictable. All someone needs to know is simply your place of birth and your date of birth. A hacker would only need to check out your social media profile on sites such as Facebook, find out these pieces of information and guess your number in as few as 1000 tries!

Here's How the Assignment of Social Security Numbers Works:

Each Social Security number begins with an "area number", a set of 3 digits denoting the state or territory where you were born, followed by 2 "group numbers" that may be any number pair from 01to 99. Last are the "serial numbers" a set of 4 sequentially handed out digits. It seems like these numbers are easily randomized and not guessable, but because these Social Security numbers are basically assigned in order, they are actually very easy to estimate. Also, most hackers know that Social Security numbers have been assigned upon application for a birth certificate, (usually 6 to 11 weeks following birth) since 1990. So if you were born after 1989, you are at very high risk of being the target of a Social Security number hack. Hackers commonly use their SSN-guessing algorithm scripts against sites that contain your credit applications.

If your Social Security number was issued after 1989, try it on yourself: If your Social Security number begins with numbers between 0001-0003, then you were likely born in New Hampshire, if it starts with numbers between 004-007, then your birth very likely took place in Maine. Hackers keep a full chart showing the states and territories associated with each Social Security number's "area code" so I've also included this chart at the back of the book, for you to try out yourself.

So What Exactly Does a Hacker Need in Order to Steal You Social Security Number?

When a hacker specifically focuses on a person for a hack, this is called a targeted hack. In order to carry out a targeted hack on you, all they require is:

- Your last name

- Your date of birth

- Knowledge of a website that you use, containing weaknesses that the hacker can exploit

At this very moment, these 3 basically open the gates for any hacker to steal your Social Security number from widely used websites.

How a Hacker Selects His or Her Target:

Hackers spend a large part of their work day scanning for vulnerable websites, seeking what is commonly known as an "in". An "in" is a flaw or security blind spot in a website that allows hackers to enter and retrieve what should be secret information.

When they find a weak spot (usually discovered in the "forgot username" retrieval function of many popularly used websites) hackers then go into the information collection stage. For example, let's say the vulnerable website that a hacker selects happens to belong to a university. Jackpot! Right there, he or she has access to a wide selection of possible targets.

Phase 1 of the Hack:

1st: The hacker will check the university's own website for any names of current or former students.

2nd: The hacker will then go through Facebook and LinkedIn for students and alumni of the university. Because people on these states often state where they went or are going to school, this immediately pulls up a large number of people to hack.

3rd: Using the names chosen on Facebook and other sites, the hacker will then check out all of those connected with them. Because many people who attend or used to attend the same school are often linked on social media, this will yield even more potential hack targets.

Phase 2 of the Hack:

Now that a pool of suitable potential hacking targets has been gathered, the hacker will then seek out and collect the following information:

1. The last name of all those chosen. This is simple as it will usually be listed on the university's website or on social media.

2. Dates of birth for all chosen. People frequently list their dates of birth on their social media profiles. Failing that the hacker can also search public records to confirm birth dates. Birth certificates can often easily be found using widely available online searching tools and this makes a hacker's job much easier as once a birth certificate application has been filed, this is the date when a Social Security number will also be assigned for all births after 1989 and before June 2011.

With the above information, the hacker is now ready to crack the targets' Social Security numbers. He or she can use this information to easily predict the first five digits of the targets' Social Security numbers. Many can do this within four attempts or less! Next, the hacker will attempt to guess the remaining four digits of the Social Security numbers, using a brute force attack where algorithms will help to try out combinations of a thousand Social Security numbers. Here, the success rate goes up to almost 90%! Bingo! The hacker has now gotten the targeted Social Security numbers and can begin his or her nefarious plan to benefit from these stolen numbers.

Don't miss the next chapter, where I'll be showing you just how a hacker can completely destroy your life, once he or she gets ahold of your Social Security number, PLUS what you can do to make sure this never happens! See you there!

Chapter 13:
What Can Hackers Really Do With Your Stolen Social Security Number?:

It happens time and time again. I come across people who are so uninformed that they don't actually believe that a stolen Social Security number is that big of threat. Although almost 1 out of every 3 Americans had their Social Security numbers hacked through the "Office of Personnel Management" hack and the "Anthem" hack during 2014 alone, the greater percentage of the population actually thinks that unless your finances are immediately tampered with or your credit score hasn't been tanked by a hacker, the hack really doesn't matter much. I'm here to tell you today that is more than just plain wrong, it's absolutely dangerous too!

Your Social Security number provides any hacker complete access to your identity and your money and just because a hacker hasn't drained your money, that doesn't mean that he or she has somehow forgotten to use your number. There are countless numbers of victims of Social Security hacking that have found out about the hack only after a long period of time. They were shocked by the news while in the middle of just living their daily lives. Some people were in the midst of trying to buy the dream home they had scrimped and saved up for over many years. These types of victims typically only find out about the hack when the bank tells them they aren't qualified for a home loan because there are numerous credit cards opened in their name , racking up thousands and thousands of dollars of unpaid debt. Every time a hacker fails to make a credit card payment, the damage ends up on YOUR credit report, leaving you unable to make large purchases or receive any credit and even make you look unappealing and irresponsible to potential employers. Even worse, this type of damage takes a long time to recover from. Unfortunately, this is actually just the tip of the iceberg when it comes to what a hacker can do with your Social Security number.

A Hacker Can Take Out A Bank Loan or Payday:

Malicious hackers are by definition, predators. They don't care about how much damage they cause, as long as it nets the m the rewards they want. Many people who have had their Social Security number hacked have found this out the hard way after hackers not only took money from their accounts and opened credit cards, but they also took out massive payday loans with their SSN. This type of move leaves hacking victims deep in the financial hole because payday loans can have an up to 400 % yearly percentage rate!

A Hacker Can Completely Drain Your Accounts:

Black hat hackers typically take everything out of their victim's savings and checking accounts but they don't stop there either. They also remove whatever they can from your individual retirement accounts and your 401(k) funds, leaving you with all of the penalties for early withdrawal of funds and none of the money you worked so hard for.

A Hacker Can Steal Your Identity and Frame You:

If a hacker commits crimes while using your Social Security number, the rap sheet is on YOU. You may face having law enforcement pulling up to your home or workplace looking for you in connection with a crime that you have absolutely NO idea about. Unfortunately, simply saying "It wasn't me." won't cut much ice with the legal system. Hackers know just how hard it is to prove that your identity was stolen and how long the investigation process can be. While you're trying to clear your name, the hacker will probably already be long gone and onto another victim!

A Hacker Can Mess With Your Medical Files:

If a hacker gets ahold of your Social Security number, they can effectively receive medical treatment under your name. This may not sound so bad but image this scenario: Your hacker receives care for a certain illness and then, when you go in to the hospital, your medical files read that you have the same disease. You end up getting treated for an illness you don't actually have, basically putting your life in serious danger!

A Hacker Can Steal Your Benefits:

A hacker can use your Social Security number in order to file for Social Security benefits or even unemployment. This leaves you in the position of not being able to get the assistance you need when you actually need it.

The Social Security Number Black Market:

Because it takes time and a great deal of effort for malicious hackers to rake in the profits from hacked Social Security numbers, they make their money on bulk sales of numbers. Each Social Security number by itself only sells for about $3 to $5. When they sell Social Security numbers in large loads, they make from $1000 to $3000 a sale. Where hackers really make money on selling your Social Security number is in the sale of something they call "Fullz."

"Fullz" are composite dossiers made up of complete credentials of one single hacking victim. These dossiers contain all of the private information you don't want a stranger to get their hands n, including your full name, mother's maiden name, your account passwords, your date of birth, address and even your place of employment. Properly prepared "Fullz" dossiers can sell for as much as $30 or $50 dollars a pop, and since hackers on average sell thousands of them at a time, they can stand to make several hundreds of thousands of dollars in one go.

If a hacker wants to make big money, however, he or she will simply use your stolen Social Security number in order to search out your medical care data and then compile it into what is known as "Kitz". "Kitz" can also include counterfeit documents (another hacker specialty) and often sell for as much as $1000 per sale. Below, you'll find a full list of the prices for all of your private information on the hacking black market.

Average Prices on the Hacking Black Market:

- Birth Dates Sell For $11 Each

- "Fullz" Dossiers (Including Social Security numbe

- American Express Credentials Sell for $7 Each

- MasterCard or Visa Credentials Sell for $4 to $5 I

- Discover Card Credentials Sell for $8 Each

- Bank Account Numbers for Bank Accounts with for $300

- Health Insurance Information Sells for $20 Per B

- Complete Identity "Kitz" Sell for $1000 to $1500

Has Your Social Security Number Been Hacked? How to Tell and How to Prevent it:

In 2015 alone, over 7% of the entire population of the United States was affected by hackers who may have potentially stolen their Social Security numbers. Millions of those affected still have no idea so it's possible that YOU may have been hacked without even knowing it.

If you ever underwent a background investigation including the submission of forms SF-8, SF-86 or SF-85P during the last 15 years, you were probably affected by the recent Social Security hacks.

Common signs that a hacker has stolen your Social Security number include financial account irregularities. I you suddenly find that you are unable to log in to your financial accounts or if our PIN code no longer gives you access to your ATM card, these are two major red flags. If your regular financial statements or bills are no longer arriving in the mail, this may indicate that a hacker has switched your address with a new one. Also, you may receive deliveries of items that you never purchased, showing that the hacker is accessing your accounts and spending your money.

Issues with Your Credit:

Remember the scenario we discussed above? If you try to purchase an automobile or make a down payment on a home and find yourself rejected, not only is it shocking, it may also indicate that your Social Security number has been hacked! Receiving a credit rejection when you have no reason to expect one is a sure sign that someone has been using access to your Social Security number to wreak havoc on your credit score. Other danger signs are seeing strange or unfamiliar charges on your credit cards, having your credit card rejected at a store or even getting phone calls from creditors asking you to pay for charges that you never made.

Tax Season Issues With the IRS:

No one likes to have run-ins with the IRS but that is exactly what you'll have if someone hacks your Social Security number. Imagine filing your taxes during tax time and being informed that a person bearing another names has also filed taxes on your Social Security number? This signals that a hacker has stolen your Social Security number and is now trying to make off with your tax refund as well.

Even worse, imagine getting an email followed by a call or letter from what you thought was the IRS, giving them your details and finding out that they were actually hackers looking for your personal information? For this reason, always confirm that you are really communicating with the real Internal Revenue Service and not an illicit hacking ring before giving away any sensitive information.

Tips for Outsmarting a Social Security Hacker:

1. Avoid being duped by a vector scam. In these scams, the hacker fishes for a reply from you by sending you an email posing as your bank, the IRS, a loan collection company or even your hospital or university. They'll ask for your details in order to "verify your identity" and if you give it to them, they easily access your Social Security number and all that it unlocks. Make sure that you trash emails like this immediately without clicking on any links or attachments and immediately report the scam to the organization the hackers were impersonating.

2. Never save any of your information on a Cloud. Even amateur hackers can crack into your Cloud in no time.

3. If you have made the mistake of opening an unknown source email, make sure you do a thorough cleanout of your device and perform a reinstall your OS (operating system) immediately.

4. Never store Your Social Security number or any personal identification, passwords or other private information or any financial information on your computer, smartphone or tablet under ANY circumstances.

5. If you store your information on an encrypted memory stick. Only use this stick on a trusted device.

6. None of these measures will matter though, if you are working on an insecure Wi-Fi network. Ensure that your network is safe before using your Social Security number for online banking etc.

7. Steer clear of sending your information to websites with known vulnerabilities such as university sites and banking sites. Hackers are scanning for these weak spots 24/7 and will find your Social Security number if you send it to these sites.

While hackers are a determined bunch and Social Security numbers are by their very nature, insecure and predictable taking these measures will discourage even the boldest hacker and make them move onto a weaker, less savvy target. Remember-Ignorance is dangerous but knowledge is always protection.

Join me in the next chapter where we'll be looking at the secrets of Wi-Fi hacking criminals and what they don't want you to know about their dangerous schemes!

Chapter 14:
Top Secrets That Wireless Hackers Don't Ever Want You To Learn!

They're everywhere, lurking inside cars in your neighborhood, casually typing into a laptop across the street or even living in the apartment or house beside you: hackers breaking into your wireless network. Wi-Fi hackers are a brand new breed: Lightening fast, technologically up-to-date and skilled in every malicious hack out there. They are the wave of the future and they may be hacking into your Wi-Fi network as you sit here reading this.

Perhaps you think this is not really a major problem. So someone is using your Wi-Fi to get a little free time online? Maybe they'll slow down your connection a little, at worst, raising your charges but other than that, what's the big deal, right?

WRONG.

While most amateur Wi-Fi hackers are simply breaking into your network in order to hitch a free internet ride at your expense, real Wi-Fi hackers have a much more sophisticated and dangerous agenda:

Because Wi-Fi hacking is essentially a fingerprint-less crime, unscrupulous hackers are drawn to it in order to carry out a whole host of nefarious activities that could end up leaving you in a very bad situation. Worse, if you are one of the many millions of people who don't properly protect your Wi-Fi network or casually use free hotspots without enough care, you are basically ASKING to be hacked.

That's why in this chapter, we'll be taking a close look at the most common Wi-Fi hacking threats AND I'll be taking you through the exact steps that malicious hackers use to break into your network. Let's get started!

Wi-Fi Hack # 1: The Sniffer Software Hack

Many malicious hackers have access to software that they can use to break into a connection and see everything that you are doing on your screen. This kind of software is called "sniffer software" and not only is it widely available online, it is also incredibly effective. Hackers use sniffer software to examine wireless router traffic and retrieve valuable information from it. If you haven't installed all necessary patches and recent updates, the hacker may be able to uncover a vulnerability in your system and exploit this weakness to "kidnap" you system and even log your every stroke with a keystroke logger!

Wi-Fi Hack # 2: The Rogue Wi-Fi Hotspot Hack

Let's say you walk into a café and after placing your order, notice that everyone around you seems to be online. You quickly realize that the café must offer free Wi-Fi and, not wanting to miss the opportunity, you pull out your own device and start seeking the network. Instantly, on your list of networks pops up a Wi-Fi hotspot, called "Free Café Wi-Fi". You obviously believe that this must be the café's free Wi-Fi and you connect to it without any suspicions. This is all perfectly safe, right?

Actually, you just committed the biggest mistake of Wi-Fi hotspot use!

Perhaps, as you are clicking away happily you don't notice the customer a few feet away at another table, busily working away on his or her own device and even if you did notice, here's nothing out of the ordinary about a customer making use of the free

Wi-Fi just like you are. What you don't see is that as you check your email, send a message to your boss, pay a few bills online, checkout your bank account statement online and maybe even fill out a form-your fellow customer is following your every move!

That "customer" is actually a malicious Wi-Fi hacking expert who has set up a fake or rogue hotspot with the name "Free Café Wi-Fi", correctly guessing that customers like you would immediately assume that this was the café's own official free Wi-Fi and that, feeling secure, you would go about your own business without fear, allowing him or her to enter your accounts, spy on your messages and basically track your every move.

By the time you pay for your coffee and leave, that hacker has already recorded your name, your email passwords and even your place of employment! If you're really unlucky, he or she may now know your bank account information and even where you live. Many who use public networks believe that there's no risk of someone accessing their personal information without alerting them. But you have to remember that your data is being transmitted to a router via radio waves and that it's literally "in the air" making it simple to intercept and capture for any hacker who wishes to do so.

Now, there's nothing harmless about that, is there?

Wi-Fi Hack #3: The Opportunistic Hack:

Malicious hackers are always on the lookout for a possible opening into your system and your information, so leaving your phone's Wi-Fi on all the time and automatically enabled presents them the perfect chance to enter. A hacker can setup an unsecure network and literally wait for victims to take the bait, just like a fisherman. If your phone's Wi-Fi is always enabled, it could connect you to that unsecure network automatically without you even realizing it and leave you vulnerable.

Risk Factors That Could Lead to a Black Hat Wi-Fi Hack:

- An open, password-free network

- Stronger WPA 2 and enabled WPS

- Network with stronger WPA encryption and weaker password

Dangers of Having Your Wi-Fi Hacked: What Malicious Hackers Can Actually Do

If a malicious hacker gets a hold of your Wi-Fi, whether through a free network, unsecured hotspot, weak password or bypassing, there really is no limit to what he or she can do. I've created this list in order to show you the most common dangers of having your Wi-Fi hacked:

- They can download illegal or copyrighted materials using YOUR Wi-Fi, in effect pinning the blame squarely on YOU!

- They can use the access point to hack into other networks illegally.

- They can retrieve sensitive or private information from hacked networks.

- They can use a "sniffer" to root out data.

- They can use the hacked network to launch Distributed Denial of Service (DDoS) campaigns against sites, while keeping his or her own tracks covered.

Hacker Tutorial: How to Hack Wi-Fi Passwords, Step-By-Step

Disclaimer: IMPORTANT!!!

I have included this Wi-Fi hacking tutorial in order to help you see just how easy it is for a hacker to crack your password and connect to your network. When knowledge is used responsibly, it can be an excellent tool to help you protect yourself, but if used in the wrong way, it can lead to all kinds of unintended negative consequences. Hacking into someone's Wi-Fi without their knowledge and permission is illegal and never bears good results, so please keep in mind that this tutorial is to help you see if you can crack the password of a friend or family member who has expressly allowed you to do so.

Now that we got that out of the way, let's get started.

Happy hacking!

Step 1: Understanding Wireless Network Security

When internet data is sent over a secured wireless connection, it's sent in encrypted packets. If you can obtain a certain networks key, you'll be able to enter the connection.

There are 2 basic kinds of encryption. These are WEP and WPA.

Wired Equivalent Privacy (WEP) Encryption:

WEP encryption is basic and is also a very insecure encryption type due to its security weaknesses. Hackers can easily crack it but this hasn't changed the fact that the majority of users still utilize it.

Wi-Fi Protected Access (WPA) Encryption:

WPA is a safer form of encryption is much safer. In order to actually crack its passphrase, you'd need to have a wordlist listing common passwords. Hackers generally have to make numerous attempts to crack it. The safest version of encryption is WPA-2 and can really only be hacked into if the user has set a popularly used password or due to the enabling of the WPA PIN. With an unusual password, it's nearly impossible to hack.

For the purposes of this tutorial, I'll clearly detail how you can crack a WEP password and access the connection.

Step 2: Items Necessary For This Hack:

CommView Software for Wi-Fi-

You'll use this to gain packets from the specific network adapter. You can download this online.

Wireless Adapter that is Compatible with CommView-

Check to see if your wireless card is compatible first. You must have this because your computer's wireless card must be compatible to allow it to enter the right mode to capture packets.

Aircrack-ng GUI Software-

Aircrack-ng GUI will crack once the packets have been captured. It's available to download online.

Time-

Depending on a variety of variables, you'll need to plan for this to take some time so don't do it for the 1st time when you're in a rush.

Step 3: CommView Setup:

- First, go the website and download the CommView file for Wi-Fi. Extract it and run the executable file setup.exe. It will provide you with driver installation instructions.

- Second, run the Software and then click the application window's play icon. This will allow you to scan for wireless networks.

- This will initiate a channel by channel scan, which will end up giving you numerous wireless network listings.

- You'll then be able to select the network you want to work on from the list.

Step 4: Choosing a Network:

- Note: Ensure that you only select a Wired Equivalent Privacy (WEP) network because that's what these steps work for.

- Go for the network with best signal strength and check the column beside it to ensure that you're getting one with the minimum dB value.

- Select your network.

Step 5: Packet Capturing:

- First, click on "Capture". This will initiate the packet capturing process from the channel.

- In order to capture packets from the network you want only, you simply:

- Go the "Rules" tab and select MAC Addresses and enable the rules.

- Choose "Capture" for "Action".

- In "Add Record" choose "Both".

- Remember that previously selected MAC address? Take it and paste it in the box below.

- Note: In order to only capture data packets, go to the top of the window and choose D from the bar.

- Next, un-select both M and C

Step 6: Packet Saving:

In order to save the packets for cracking, first click to make auto saving possible at the logging tab.

Next go to Maximum Directory Size and Ensure that it's set at 2000 then head to Average Log File Size and make that 20.

Step 7: The Capture Process:

- It's important to keep in mind that the data packet capturing process can take a bit of time. This is because you'll need at least 100,000 packets captured for this to work out.(Again, the signal strength decides everything.).

- Once you've reached this number of captured packets it's time for exportation. To do this:

- Click on concatenate logs on the log tab and choose all saved logs.

- Keep CommView for Wi-Fi open and head to the folder with the concatenated logs saved in it.

- In the log file, choose the following: File and then Export and then the Wire Shark tcpdump format.

- At this point, select a destination to save the logs bearing the.cap extension there.

Step 8: The Cracking Process Begins:

Extract zip file from your download of Aircrack-ng **before heading to "bin".**

- After running Aircrack-ng GUI, select the WEP option (Wireless Equivalent Privacy).

- Go to the previously saved .cap file.

- Open and "Launch" it, then type your selected network's index number into the command prompt. This will result in a certain waiting period and then the wireless key should appear for you. Congratulations!!!You've just successfully cracked WEP Wi-Fi!! Now that you see just how easy it is to follow these steps, you can easily see the need to make sure that malicious hackers aren't hacking into your network.

With that in mind, let's take a look at the top ways to secure your Wi-Fi and ensure that you are hacker-free:

What You Need to Do to Stay Safe on Public Wi-Fi Networks:

http://lifehacker.com/5576927/how-to-stay-safe-on-public-wi-fi-networks

As we discussed earlier in this section, there are huge risks associated with using public Wi-Fi networks because even when these networks are secured with passwords, the fact remains that your data could potentially be at risk from many other strangers on the network with you. Here are some essential tips to keep you your device and your data safe as you connect on public Wi-Fi networks.

Settings to Enable or Adjust:

Turn Off Sharing:

Make sure you disable sharing whenever you use Wi-Fi on a public network because leaving it turned on will make all of your data vulnerable to the prying eyes of hackers.

To Turn Off Sharing In OS X: Head to System Preferences, then Sharing and untick all of the boxes.

While there, also disable network discovery, making it impossible for strangers to spot your device and keeping you much safer. Go to Stealth Mode in the Advanced Settings of your firewall to do so in OS X.

To Turn Off Sharing In Windows: Go to the Control Panel, Head to Network and Internet and then Network and Sharing Center. From there, select Change Advanced Sharing Settings, switch off printer sharing, file sharing, public folder sharing and network discovery. To do so in Windows, go to advanced shared settings and untick the box.

Switch Off Your Wi-Fi When You're Not On it:

One of the main ways people expose themselves to hacks is to leave the Wi-Fi on when not necessary so keep safe by clicking off. Whether you're on Windows or using OS X, you can do this in just seconds. If you're using a Mac, head to the menu bar, select the Wi-Fi icon and choose turn off AirPort. For Windows, simply head to the task bar and click the Wi-Fi icon to switch off. Switching off your Wi-Fi when not in use will ensure that you're not attracting the attention of hackers unnecessarily.

Turn Your Firewall On:

Your firewall is your first line of defense against Wi-Fi hacks. Keep your default firewall switched on to keep hackers out. Check by heading to Windows under Control Panel > System and Security > Windows Firewall;

For a Mac, head to System Preferences > Security & Privacy > Firewall and ensuring that it's switched on.

Go For HTTPS and SSL:

Malicious hackers can "sniff" normal web traffic over HTTP wireless networks and if this traffic includes sensitive information like your passwords, it could lead to serious security issues for you. Enable SSL for internet-accessing applications or employ HTTPS when going on sites. This will ensure that all data transferring from your computer to the internet and vice versa is encrypted and therefore unreadable.

Always look to see that the https in the address bar of any site you're on includes the letter "s" at its end as this indicates that you're on HTTPS.

Secure sites such as Gmail and others employ HTTPS by default but when on other sites, make sure that the letter "s" doesn't go away. If you don't see it on the address bar, log out of the site you're on right away. While many sites automatically use HTTP, you can always put HTTPS in the address bar and see if it will still work.

Always make sure that you only do normal browsing on a public network and avoid going on your bank's site or any other site requiring you to input private information, to be extra sure of safety.

When it comes to SSL encryption, only use email desktop clients that support SSL encryption because failing to do so when on a public network could mean that your sensitive information is immediately visible to a hacker who can then steal it all.

Choose a VPN (Virtual Private Network)

SSL encryption may not be supported on all sites that you use so instead, use a VPN in order to makes sure that despite being on a public network, all of your browsing is routed through a private network. There are plenty of free, effective Virtual Private Networks available online so simply choose one and install it to keep yourself secure on public wireless networks.

Use Encryption:

Protect yourself by going on sites that encrypt or when using non-encrypting sites, always download the encryption software that reputable sites often provide. Keep in mind that 55% of the most popular websites don't offer encryption, meaning that any data is viewable by potential hackers. Check your browser for an indication of whether or not the site you're visiting has data encryption.

Use a 4G-Powered Personal Hotspot:

If you travel often it may be worth getting a 4G-powered personal hotspot. It offers you your very own cellular connection that you can employ a secure password on in the same way that your home network is also secured.

Never Use Public Wi-Fi that Is Not Protected with a Password:

If you are in the position of needing to frequently utilize public Wi-Fi, it is really important that you always steer clear of Wi-Fi networks that are not secured and protected. At the very least, never make online financial transactions or enter personal information such as your Social Security number over a public wireless connection. You have to remember that the average hacker can break into these networks very quickly and with minimal ease. This is no idle threat- banks in recent years have lost over $900 million from these malicious hackers and you don't want YOUR money to be a part of that figure.

How to Protect Your Home Network From Wi-Fi Hackers:

It's more important than ever to secure your Wi-Fi connection from unknown outsiders. If your Wi-Fi network is constantly playing host to strangers who are using it for their own means, you MUST act now!

In recent years there have been a spate of arrests in which innocent people were charged for sending hate mail or downloading illegal, copyrighted material from the internet. These people were not guilty of the crimes they were arrested for. Instead, unscrupulous black hat hackers used the Wi-Fi networks of these innocent people to carry out illegal activities and covered their own tracks, while leaving the unsuspecting Wi-Fi network owners in big legal trouble. You can never imagine how hard it is to convince law enforcement officials that it wasn't you when all of the malicious traffic points to your door!

Using this step-by-step safety protocol will help you to ensure that unwanted intruders never piggyback on your connection and that malicious hackers stay well away from your personal Wi-Fi network.

1st: Head to Your Router Settings Page:

In order to access your wireless router's settings type the following into your web browser: "192.168.1.1". Next, enter the right password and username for the router. This can vary from router to router so if it doesn't work for yours, simply check your router's manual or look it up for your router type.

2nd: Create a Password:

After logging into your router, now it's time to change the password. Most people still have the default password that the router first came with and this makes for a very unsafe situation. Malicious hackers have updated lists of the common factory-set default passwords for various routers. Changing it to a unique password will help to keep hackers out of your router and increase your Wi-Fi's security. To change it, go to the Administration settings on the router's settings.

3rd: Switch The Name of Your Network's SSID:

Your wireless router's Wireless Network Name or SSID is frequently set to the name of the router type, such as Linksys etc. Changing the name will help to ensure that you connect to the right network among many choices. **NOTE:** Never create a SSID name using any private information such as your first or last name or address.

4th: Network Encryption Enabling:

Encrypting your wireless signals can make sure that other devices in your vicinity aren't piggybacking onto your personal internet connection. Encryption forms include Wireless Equivalent Protocol (WEP), Wi-Fi Protected Access (WPA) WPA-Personal and WPA2.

As we know, WEP is much less secure while WPA versions are much safer but usage depends on the year of your device's make. In order to enable encryption of your wireless network, first head to your routers configuration page and open up the wireless security settings. Doing so should allow you to choose your preferred method of security. Here you have to make the next move based on your device's age. If your device was made after 2006, you can choose WPA2. For devices made before 2006, WEP is your choice. Choose a unique and hard to guess passphrase and set it to access the network. Malicious hackers often break into WEP and WPA keys using freely available tools like AirCrack.

5th: MAC Address Filtering:

All wireless devices have a specific MAC address in the same way that PCs on the internet have specific IP addresses. To create even more security or yourself, go ahead and add the specific MAC addresses of your devices to your wireless router's settings. This will effectively bar any non-specified devices from using your network.

Although it is not unheard of for hackers to spoof your MAC address, they would first have to be aware of a MAC address of a device connected to your network in order to pull this spoof off.

In order to filter MAC Addresses: List all the devices you will allow to connect to your network. Once you have their MAC addresses, add this list to your router's administrative settings' MAC address filtering section. Tip: To figure out your devices' MAC addresses, simply open up Command Prompt, type in "ipconfig /all". You will now be able to see the MAC address next to "Physical Address". When it comes to wireless devices' MAC addresses, these should show up under network settings.

<u>Note:</u> If you want to allow someone you know to connect to your network, find and add their device's MAC address to your router. If it's just for brief period of time, you can then remove the new MAC address after the person no longer needs to connect to your network.

Unfortunately, those wily hackers can still get around this measure to a certain extent using a sniffer such as Nmap to find out your device's MAC address. He or she can then change his or her own device's MAC address to match yours, through a free tool like MAC Shift.

6th: Shorten your Wireless Signals' Range:

A major risk factor for having your Wi-Fi hacked is having an over-long wireless signal range. Think about reducing your signal's range by either utilizing a different wireless channel or by switching you router's mode from 802.11n or 802.11b to 802.11g. Another method is to actually move the router's physical location by placing it within a box, under a bed or even try wrapping the router's antennas with foil to reduce the signal's reach.

If this doesn't work for you, consider applying a coat of anti-Wi-Fi paint to block the signal, not allowing it to escape and be accessed by strangers. Painting the room in which your router sits with this paint means that the chemicals within the paint will actually form a physical barrier, trapping your signal in the room and keeping any would-be hackers out.

7th: Do a Router Firmware Update:

Always check the website of your router's manufacturer periodically, in order to make sure that you're running the most recent firmware updates. In order to discover what version of firmware you are currently running, you can go to the routers dashboard at 192.168.

8th: Connect

Now, it's time to wrap up the security process. After enabling all of the security settings for your router, add them to all of your devices in order to allow them to access the network. Choose to let your computer connect automatically, to reduce the hassle of having to enter the passphrase, SSID etc. all the time.

Your wireless network is now close to being hack-proof, your data is much safer and you've just made any potential Wi-Fi hacker's job a lot tougher!

Conclusion:
The Takeaway

Congratulations! You've completed this guide on the dark side of the hacking world and hopefully, you've learned a lot about this shadowy, murky and often downright dangerous world that you didn't previously know. As I explained in the opening sections of this book, the real purpose of learning about the secrets of malicious hackers behind their screens and the methods, motivations and mindsets that they use and possess, is not about blind panic. It's not about fear, or feeling so insecure online that you feel you can never confidently use your devices. In fact, it's all about the exact opposite. Knowledge instead of blind panic, security and confidence instead of fear- these are the goals I started with when I set out to write this book.

Instead of looking at it as a horror story of all the things that could possibly go wrong involving hackers, I want you to use it as a clear, honest and revealing guide that can help you steer yourself AWAY from potential risks. Whenever you're facing a possible security threat, are wondering whether or not to open that email, click that link, post that private detail about you on social media or any of the other numerous risk factors I've explained in this book, don't hesitate to go back and flip to the chapter that describes the situation you're facing. Take a look at the warning signs, the common tricks hackers use in connection with your scenario and the ways to prevent and defend against a hacking attack. Go through the steps of the hacking tutorials I shared with you and remind yourself of just how easily a hacker can infiltrate your system AND THEN make your choice. Believe me, you'll find the information to be extremely helpful in keeping yourself, your device, system, and your network protected.

In closing, I'd like to thank you for joining me as I brought to light the dark side of the hacking world, but I'd also like to remind you that not all hacking is bad hacking. There are many creative, harmless and indeed, even useful ways that non-malicious ethical hackers utilize hacking skills.

But while there is no reason for paranoia, there is also no denying that malicious black hat hacking is rapidly gaining power and with so much of our lives lived online, with so many of our details and the details of our loved ones stored on our devices and with our identities, privacy, security and safety at risk each and every single time we log on, learning about the mysterious and often very damaging tactics of malicious hackers is absolutely necessary.

I'd like to leave you with these words: Knowledge is power and in order to beat your enemy, you must know your enemy. In the fight against hacking campaigns, keeping yourself aware is the ONLY way to keep yourself safe!

Stay Alert, Stay Protected and Stay Well!

P.S. Make sure you check out the useful index I've attached at the end of this book, containing commonly used hacking terms you need to know and even a replica of the kind of chart hackers use to figure out their targets Social Security numbers.

INDEX

Hacker Terminology Guide: Know the Lingo, Understand the Process

As you've seen throughout this book, hacking is a very technical subject and a lot of the terms associated with it are difficult to decipher. That's why I've put together this glossary of the most important and commonly used hacking terms you need to know, in order to fully understand the world of hacking.

Adware: Adware can refer to either software that brings up ads within a usually free program OR more frequently, a type of spyware that secretly tracks your browsing and brings up ads according to the information it obtains.

Back door: Back door (sometimes also called a trap door) refers to a secret entry into a device or software Backdoors get past password protections, logins and other security measures.

Black hat hacker: A black hat hacker is a hacker who hacks or "cracks" illegally and for illicit purposes, ranging from destruction and revenge to more commonly, financial benefits. Black hat hackers perform hacks that cause damage and sometimes unleash very negative effects.

Botnet: Botnet refers to a chain of devices that have effectively been "enslaved" by a malicious black hat hacker. The hacker then uses these devices to launch DoS (denial of service) campaigns and spam against a chosen target. This is achieved through the use of a malware infection.

Brute force attack: Hackers often use these exhaustive key searches and they basically refer to an automatic search for every single possible password for a system. These searches are often much less time effective and inefficient than more advanced hacking methods and they are only chosen when no other method is available. However, they can be made more efficient by narrowing down the range of password types.

Clone phishing: Clone phishing refers to the process of modifying a real email by adding an illegitimate link in order to elicit private information from the recipient.

Code: Code refers to instructions that rule a program or device. These instructions are often text-based and can read by machines. Code-changes can lead to changes in the program or device that the code governs.

Cracking: Cracking refers to the process of illegally or illicitly breaking into a computer system, usually with the intent to cause damage or to benefit financially.

Denial of service attack (DoS): DoS refers to a method that hackers employ against a certain target, whether a network or a site, that is meant to bring it down temporarily, usually by overwhelming it with a massive wave of content request.

Distributed denial of service attack (DDoS): This refers to a DoS that utilizes numerous devices, using a number of separate machines. This is often done by infecting many devices with Trojans and then corralling them into a botnet network.

Firewall: A system using hardware, software, or both to prevent unauthorized access to a system or machine.

Gray hat: Just like the rest of life, hacking is often less black or white than it is gray. The term gray hat hacker reflects that reality. A gray hat hacker will break the law in the pursuit of a hack, but does not do so maliciously or for personal gain. Many would argue Anonymous are gray hats

IP: An IP or internet protocol address is the specific numeric fingerprint belonging to each device on an Internet Protocol network. The IP can work as a locater and an identifier of the user on the device. Hackers regularly use port scanning against devices, using knowledge of IPs.

Keystroke logging: Keystroke logging refers to the process of "watching" the keys being pressed on a device. Malicious hackers can use this process to find out users' passwords, login IDs and other sensitive information. Hackers frequently send out phishing emails to targets which then install Trojans containing keystroke loggers.

Malware: Malware refers to a type of software program that is created in order to retrieve or steal information from a device, take the device over completely or cause it to be damaged. Adware, spyware, keyloggers, rootkits, viruses and others are all malware.

Payload: Payload refers to the portion of a virus that is responsible for taking over a device, damaging or destroying information, retrieving information or other activities.

Packet sniffer: A packet sniffer is a program made to find and take specific data, including passwords and other personal information.

Phishing: Phishing refers to the method of fooling a user into handing over private, sensitive information. It is accomplished by impersonating trustworthy legitimate individuals or organizations through phishing emails and fake sites.

Rootkit: Rootkit refers to a software program set that hackers use to obtain high-level entry, in order to introduce malware into a system while disguising the attack.

Script kiddie: Script kiddie is used to disparagingly refer to inexperienced wannabe hacker/crackers who lack real skills and who usually use already created tools to cause damage and to build up reputations as pseudo-hackers.

Social engineering: Social engineering refers to the process of using psychological insights and an understanding of human nature and cognitive biases to dupe people into handing over private information.

Spoofing: Spoofing refers to the process of changing an email's header, in order to suggest that it has a different origin. For example, a malicious hacker can modify the header of his or her email to make you believe that it is from the spoofing target's credit card company. Computers can be spoofed too, as hackers use IP spoofing, a process of modifying an IP, to make it appear to be a legitimate and reliable host.

Spyware: This is a kind of malware that lurks on a server or device and relays information such as passwords, IDs and bank account numbers back to the master server.

Trojan horse: A Trojan refers to a kind of malware that disguises itself as trustworthy, useful or interesting software. Once it gains entry, it frequently places a backdoor on the targeted device.

Virus: A virus is a kind of malware that replicates and places these replications of itself into infected devices. It has the ability to retrieve private information, allow for keystroke logging, and damage a hard drive, among other destructive actions.

Vulnerability: Vulnerabilities are areas of weakness that are exploitable, allowing hackers an "in" into a device.

White hat hacker: This refers to a hacker without malice, or an ethical hacker. White hats typically utilize their hacking know-how positively, often uncovering weaknesses that malicious hackers could use to gain illegal entry and helping individuals and organizations to protect themselves from these hacks.

Zero day exploit: This refers to a never-been –used before weakness or unexploited vulnerability in a system.

****

A Hacker's Guide to Social Security Number Area Codes: I've included this chart to highlight just how easy it is for hackers to crack your Social Security number based on the address of birth!

Disclaimer: Please keep in mind that utilizing another person's Social Security number is illegal. This chart was included for informational and illustrative purposes only.

001-003 New Hampshire

004-007 Maine

008-009 Vermont

010-034 Massachusetts

035-039 Rhode Island

040-049 Connecticut

050-134 New York

135-158 New Jersey

159-211 Pennsylvania

212-220 Maryland

221-222 Delaware

223-231 Virginia

691-699

232-236 West Virginia

232 North Carolina

237-246

681-690

247-251 South Carolina

654-658

252-260 Georgia

667-675

261-267 Florida

589-595

766-772

268-302 Ohio

303-317 Indiana

318-361 Illinois

362-386 Michigan

387-399 Wisconsin

400-407 Kentucky

408-415 Tennessee

756-763

416-424 Alabama

425-428 Mississippi

587-588

752-755

429-432 Arkansas

676-679

433-439 Louisiana

659-665

440-448 Oklahoma

449-467 Texas

627-645

468-477 Minnesota

478-485 Iowa

486-500 Missouri

501-502 North Dakota

503-504 South Dakota

505-508 Nebraska

509-515 Kansas

516-517 Montana

518-519 Idaho

520 Wyoming

521-524 Colorado

650-653

525, 585 New Mexico

648-649

526-527 Arizona

600-601

764-765

528-529 Utah

646-647

530, 680 Nevada

531-539 Washington

540-544 Oregon

545-573 California

602-626

574 Alaska

575-576 Hawaii

750-751

577-579 District of Columbia

580 Virgin Islands

580-584 Puerto Rico

596-599

586 Guam

586 American Samoa

586 Philippine Islands

www.ingramcontent.com/pod-product-compliance
Lightning Source LLC
Chambersburg PA
CBHW071114050326
40690CB00008B/1219

* 9 7 8 1 5 2 2 9 4 0 6 8 5 *